Selected Poems

Selected Poems

Mona Van Duyn

Alfred A. Knopf

NEW YORK

2002

THIS IS A BORZOI BOOK
PUBLISHED BY ALFRED A. KNOPF

www.randomhouse.com/knopf/poetry

Knopf, Borzoi Books, and the colophon are registered trademarks of Random House, Inc.

Valentines to the Wide World: copyright © 1942, 1944, 1953, 1954, 1956, 1957, 1958, 1959
by Mona Van Duyn (The Cummington Press)
A Time of Bees: copyright © 1960, 1962, 1963, 1964 by Mona Van Duyn
(University of North Carolina Press)
To See, To Take: copyright © 1964, 1965, 1966, 1967, 1968, 1969, 1970, 1971
by Mona Van Duyn (Atheneum)
Bedtime Stories: copyright © 1972, 1973 by Mona Van Duyn (Ceres Press)
Merciful Disguises: copyright © 1966, 1968, 1969, 1970, 1971, 1972, 1973
by Mona Van Duyn (Atheneum)
Letters from a Father, and Other Poems: copyright © 1982 by Mona Van Duyn (Atheneum)
Near Changes: copyright © 1983, 1986, 1987, 1988, 1989, 1990 by Mona Van Duyn
(Alfred A. Knopf)
If It Be Not I: Collected Poems 1959–1982: copyright © 1993 by Mona Van Duyn
(Alfred A. Knopf)
Firefall: copyright © 1993 by Mona Van Duyn (Alfred A. Knopf)

Library of Congress Cataloging-in-Publication Data
Van Duyn, Mona.
[Poems. Selections]
Selected poems / by Mona Van Duyn.
p. cm.
ISBN 0-375-41369-3
I. Title.
PS3543 A563 A6 2002
811'.54—dc21   2001050672

Manufactured in the United States of America
First Edition

Contents

To See, To Take   1970

Bedtime Stories   1972

New Poems from Merciful Disguises   *1973*

Letters from a Father, and Other Poems   *1982*

Near Changes   *1990*

Firefall   *1993*

Valentines to the
Wide World

1959

Three Valentines to the Wide World

I

The child disturbs our view. Tow-head bent, she
stands on one leg and folds up the other. She is listening
to the sound of her fingernail on a scab on her knee.
If I were her mother I would think right now of the chastening
that ridiculous arrangement of bones and bumps must go through,
and that big ear too, till they learn what to do and hear.
People don't perch like something seen in a zoo
or in tropical sections of Florida. They'll have to buy her
a cheap violin if she wants to make scraping noises.
She is eight years old. What in the world could she wear
that would cover her hinges and disproportions? Her face is
pointed and blank, the brows as light as the hair.

"Mother, is love God's hobby?" At eight you don't even
look up from your scab when you ask it. A kid's squeak,
is that a fit instrument for such a question?
Eight times the seasons turned and cold snow tricked
the earth to death, and still she hasn't noticed.
Her friend has a mean Dad, a milkman always kicks
at the dog, but by some childish hocus-pocus
she blinks them away. She counts ten and sucks in her cheeks
and the globe moves under the green thumb of an Amateur,
the morning yelp, the crying at recess are gone.
In the freeness of time He gardens, and to His leisure
old stems entrust new leaves all winter long.

Hating is hard work, and the uncaring thought is hard;
but loving is easy, love is that lovely play
that makes us and keeps us? No one answers you. Such absurd
charity of the imagination has shamed us, Emily.
I remember now. Legs shoved you up, you couldn't tell

3

where the next tooth would fall out or grow in, or what
your own nose would look like next year. Anything was possible.
Then it slowed down, and you had to keep what you got.
When this child's body stretches to the grace of her notion,
and she's tamed and curled, may she be free enough to bring
mind and heart to that serious recreation
where anything is still possible—or almost anything.

II

I have never enjoyed those roadside overlooks from which
you can see the mountains of two states. The view keeps generating
a kind of pure, meaningless exaltation
that I can't find a use for. It drifts away from things.

And it seems to me also that the truckdriver's waste of the world
is sobering. When he rolls round it on a callus of macadam,
think how all those limping puppydogs, girls
thumbing rides under the hot sun, or under the white moon

how all those couples kissing at the side of the road,
bad hills, cat eyes, and horses asleep on their feet
must run together into a statement so abstract
that it's tiresome. Nothing in particular holds still in it.

Perhaps he does learn that the planet can still support life,
though with some difficulty. Or even that there is injustice,
since he rolls round and round and may be able to feel
the slight but measurable wobble of the earth on its axis.

But what I find most useful is the poem. To find some spot
on the surface and then bear down until the skin can't stand
the tension and breaks under it, breaks under that half-demented
"pressure of speech" the psychiatrists saw in Pound,

is a discreetness of consumption that I value. Only the poem
is strong enough to make the initial rupture,
at least for me. Its view is simultaneous
discovery and reminiscence. It starts with the creature

and stays there, assuming creation is worth the time
it takes, from the first day down to the last line on the last page.
And I've never seen anything like it for making you think
that to spend your life on such old premises is a privilege.

III

Your yen two wol slee me sodenly;
I may the beautee of hem not sustene.
MERCILES BEAUTE

When, in the middle of my life, the earth stalks me
with sticks and stones, I fear its merciless beauty.
This morning a bird woke me with a four-note outcry,
and cried out eighteen times. With the shades down, sleepy
as I was, I recognized his agony.
It resembles ours. With one more heave, the day
sends us a generous orb and lets us see
all sights lost when we lie down finally.

And if, in the middle of her life, some beauty falls on
a girl, who turns under its swarm to astonished woman,
then, into that miraculous buzzing, stung
in the lips and eyes without mercy, strangers may run.
An untended power—I pity her and them.
It is late, late; haste! says the falling moon,
as blinded they stand and smart till the fever's done
and blindly she moves, wearing her furious weapon.

Beauty is merciless and intemperate.
Who, turning this way and that, by day, by night,

still stands in the heart-felt storm of its benefit,
will plead in vain for mercy, or cry, "Put out
the lovely eyes of the world, whose rise and set
move us to death!" And never will temper it,
but against that rage slowly may learn to pit
love and art, which are compassionate.

The Gentle Snorer

When summer came, we locked up our lives and fled
to the woods in Maine, and pulled up over our heads
a comforter filled with batts of piney dark,
tied with crickets' chirretings and the *bork*
of frogs; we hid in a sleep of strangeness from
the human humdrum.

A pleasant noise the unordered world makes wove
around us. Burrowed, we heard the scud of waves,
wrack of bending branch, or plop of a fish
on his heavy home; the little beasts rummaged the brush.
We dimmed to silence, slipped from the angry pull
of wishes and will.

And then we had a three-week cabin guest
who snored; he broke the wilderness of our rest.
As all night long he sipped the succulent air,
that rhythm we shared made visible to the ear
a rich refreshment of the blood. We fed in
unison with him.

A sound we dreamed and woke to, over the snuff
of wind, not loud enough to scare off the roof
the early morning chipmunks. Under our skins
we heard, as after disease, the bright, thin
tick of our time. Sleeping, he mentioned death
and celebrated breath.

He went back home. The water flapped the shore.
A thousand bugs drilled at the darkness. Over
the lake a loon howled. Nothing spoke up for us,
salvagers always of what we have always lost;
and we thought what the night needed was more of man,
he left us so partisan.

Woman Waiting

Over the gray, massed blunder of her face
light hung crudely and apologetic sight
crossed in a hurry. Asking very little,
her eyes were patiently placed there.
Dress loved nothing and wandered away
wherever possible, needing its own character.

Used to the stories, we wise children
made pleasant pictures of her when alive, till
someone who knew told us it was never so.

Next, wisely waited to see the hidden dancer,
the expected flare leaping through that fog
of flesh, but no one ever did.
In a last wisdom, conceived of a moment
love lit her like a star and the star burned out.
Interested friends said this had never happened.

Death by Aesthetics

Here is the doctor, an abstracted lover,
dressed as a virgin, coming to keep the tryst.
The patient was early; she is lovely; but yet
she is sick, his instruments will agree on this.

Is this the place, she wonders, and is he the one?
Yes, love is the healer, he will strip her bare,
and all his machinery of definition
tells her experience is costly here,

so she is reassured. The doctor approaches
and bends to her heart. But she sees him sprout like a tree
with metallic twigs on his fingers and blooms of chrome
at his eye and ear for the sterile ceremony.

Oh tight and tighter his rubber squeeze of her arm.
"Ahhh" she sighs at a chilly touch on her tongue.
Up the tubes her breath comes crying, as over her,
back and breast, he moves his silver thumb.

His fluoroscope hugs her. Soft the intemperate girl,
disordered. Willing she lies while he unfolds
her disease, but a stem of glass protects his fingertips
from her heat, nor will he catch her cold.

He peels her. Under the swaddling epiderm
her body is the same blue bush. Beautiful canals
course like a postcard scene that's sent him often.
He counts the *tiptup, tiptup* of her dutiful valves.

Pain hides like a sinner in her mesh of nerves.
But her symptoms constellate! Quickly he warms
to his consummation, while her fever flares
in its wick of vein, her wicked blood burns.

He hands her a paper. "Goodbye. Live quietly,
make some new friends. I've seen these stubborn cases
cured with time. My bill will arrive. Dear lady,
it's been a most enjoyable diagnosis."

She clings, but her fingers slip on his starchy dress.
"Don't leave me! Learn me! If this is all, you've swindled
my whole booty of meaning, where is my dearness?
Pore against pore, the delicate hairs commingled,

with cells and ligaments, tissue lapped on bone,
meet me, feel the way my body feels,
and in my bounty of dews, fluxes and seasons,
orifices, in my wastes and smells

see self. Self in the secret stones I chafed
to shape in my bladder. Out of a dream I fished
the ache that feeds in my stomach's weedy slough.
This tender swelling's the bud of my frosted wish.

Search out my mind's embroidery of scars.
My ichor runs to death so speedily,
spit up your text and taste my living texture.
Sweat to hunt me with love, and burn with me."

But he is gone. "Don't touch me" was all he answered.
"Separateness," says the paper. The world, we beg,
will keep her though she's caught its throbbing senses,
its bugs still swim in her breath, she's bright with its plague.

A Relative and an Absolute

It has been cool so far for December, but of course the cold doesn't last long down here. The Bible is being fulfilled so rapidly that it looks like it won't be long until Jesus will come in the air, with a shout, and all those who have accepted Jesus as their own personal Saviour will be caught up to meet him and then that terrible war will be on earth. The battle of Armageddon. And all the unsaved people will have to go through the great tribulation. Hope you are both well. Bye.

An aunt, my down-to-earth father's sibling, went to stay
in Texas, and had to continue by mail, still thanklessly,
her spiritual supervision of the family.

Texas orchards are fruitful. A card that would portray
this fact in green and orange, and even more colorfully say
on its back that Doom is nearly upon us, came regularly

at birthday, Easter and Christmas—and sometimes between the three.
That the days passed, and the years, never bothered her prophecy;
she restressed, renewed and remailed its imminence faithfully.

Most preaching was wrong, she felt, but found for her kin on Sunday,
in one voice on one radio station, one truth for all to obey.
Salvation being thus limited, it seemed to me

there was something unpleasant about that calm tenacity
of belief that so many others would suffer catastrophe
at any moment. She seemed too smug a protégée.

Otherwise, I rather liked her. Exchanging a recipe
or comparing winters with neighbors, she took life quietly
in a stuffy bungalow, among doilies of tatting and crochet.

She had married late, and enjoyed the chance to baby
a husband, to simmer the wholesome vegetables and see
that vitamins squeezed from his fruit were drunk without delay.

Though she warned of cities and churches and germs, some modesty
or decorum, when face to face with us, wouldn't let her convey
her vision of Armageddon. But the postcards set it free.

It was hovering over the orange groves, she need only lay
her sewing aside, and the grandeur and rhythm of its poetry
came down and poured in her ear, her pencil moved eloquently.

She wrote it and wrote it. She will be "caught up," set free from
    her clay
as Christ comes "with a shout in the air" and trumpeting angels play,
and "the terrible war will be on earth" on that Judgment Day,

expecting all those years her extinction of body would be
attended by every creature, wrapped round in the tragedy
of the world, in its pandemonium and ecstasy.

When she died last winter, several relatives wrote to say
a kidney stone "as big as a peach pit" took her away.
Reading the letters, I thought, first of all, of the irony,

then, that I myself, though prepared to a certain degree,
will undoubtedly feel, when I lie there, as lonesome in death as she
and just as surprised at its trivial, domestic imagery.

A Kind of Music

When consciousness begins to add diversity to its intensity, its value is no longer absolute and inexpressible. The felt variations in its tone are attached to the observed movement of its objects; in these objects its values are embedded. A world loaded with dramatic values may thus arise in imagination; terrible and delightful presences may chase one another across the void; life will be a kind of music made by all the senses together. Many animals probably have this kind of experience.

SANTAYANA

Irrelevance characterizes the behavior of our puppy.
In the middle of the night he decides that he wants to play,
runs off when he's called, when petted is liable to pee,
cowers at a twig and barks at his shadow or a tree,
grins at intruders and bites us in the leg suddenly.

No justification we humans have been able to see
applies to his actions. While we go by the time of day,
or the rules, or the notion of purpose or consistency,
he follows from moment to moment a sensuous medley
that keeps him both totally subject and totally free.

I'll have to admit, though, we've never been tempted to say
that he jumps up to greet us or puts his head on our knee
or licks us or lies at our feet irrelevantly.
When it comes to loving, we find ourselves forced to agree
all responses are reasons and no reason is necessary.

Toward a Definition of Marriage

I

It is to make a fill, not find a land.
Elsewhere, often, one sights americas of awareness,
suddenly there they are, natural and anarchic,
with plantings scattered but rich, powers to be harnessed—
but this is more like building a World's Fair island.
Somebody thought it could be done, contracts are signed,
and now all materials are useful, everything; sludge
is scooped up and mixed with tin cans and fruit rinds,
even tomato pulp and lettuce leaves are solid
under pressure. Presently the ground humps up and shows.
But this marvel of engineering is not all.
A hodgepodge of creatures (no bestiary would suppose
such an improbable society) are at this time
turned loose to run on it, first shyly, then more free,
and must keep, for self's sake, wiles, anger, much of their
spiny or warted nature, yet learn courtesy.

II

It is closest to picaresque, but essentially artless.
If there were any experts, they are dead, it takes too long.
How could its structure be more than improvising,
when it never ends, but line after line plods on,
and none of the ho-hum passages can be skipped?
It has a bulky knowledge, but what symbol comes anywhere near
suggesting it? No, the notion of art won't fit it—
unless—when it's embodied. For digression there
is meaningful, and takes such joy in the slopes and crannies
that every bony gesture is generous, full,
all lacy with veins and nerves. There, the spirit
smiles in its skin, and impassions and sweetens to style.

14

So this comes to resemble a poem found in his notebooks
after the master died. A charred, balky man, yet one day
as he worked at one of those monuments, the sun guiled him,
and he turned to a fresh page and simply let play
his great gift on a small ground. Yellowed, unpublished,
he might have forgotten he wrote it. (All this is surmise.)
But it's known by heart now; it rounded the steeliest shape
to shapeliness, it was so loving an exercise.

III

Or, think of it as a duel of amateurs.
These two have almost forgot how it started—in an alley,
impromptu, and with a real affront. One thought,
"He is not me," and one, "She is not me,"
and they were coming toward each other with sharp knives
when someone saw it was illegal, dragged them away,
bundled them into some curious canvas clothing,
and brought them to this gym that is almost dark, and empty.
Now, too close together for the length of the foils,
wet with fear, they dodge, stumble, strike,
and if either finally thinks he would rather be touched
than touch, he still must listen to the clang and tick
of his own compulsive parrying. Endless. Nothing
but a scream for help can make the authorities come.
If it ever turns into more of a dance than a duel,
it is only because, feeling more skillful, one
or the other steps back with some notion of grace
and looks at his partner. Then he is able to find
not a wire mask for his target, but a red heart
sewn on the breast like a simple valentine.

IV

If there's a Barnum way to show it, then think back
to a climax in the main tent. At the foot of the bleachers, a road
encloses the ringed acts; consider that as its design,
and consider whoever undertakes it as the whole parade
which, either as preview or summary, assures the public
hanging in hopeful suspense between balloons and peanutshells
that it's all worthwhile. The ponies never imagined
anything but this slow trot of ribbons and jinglebells.
An enormous usefulness constrains the leathery bulls
as they stomp on, and hardly ever run amok.
The acrobats practised all their lives for this easy
contortion, and clowns are enacting a necessary joke
by harmless zigzags in and out of line.
But if the procession includes others less trustworthy?
When they first see the circle they think some ignorant
cartographer has blundered. The route is a lie,
drawn to be strict but full, drawn so each going forth
returns, returns to a more informed beginning.
And still a familiar movement might tempt them to try it,
but since what they know is not mentioned in the tromboning
of the march, neither the daylong pace of caged
impulse, nor the hurtle of night's terrible boxcars,
they shrink in their stripes and refuse; other performers
drive them out and around with whips and chairs.
They never tame, but may be taught to endure
the illusion of tameness. Year after year their paws
pad out the false curve, and their reluctant parading
extends the ritual's claim to its applause.

V

Say, for once, that the start is a pure vision
like the blind man's (though he couldn't keep it, trees
soon bleached to familiar) when the bandage came off
and what a world could be first fell on his eyes.
Say it's when campaigns are closest to home
that farsighted lawmakers oftenest lose their way.
And repeat what everyone knows and nobody wants
to remember, that always, always expediency
must freckle the fairest wishes. Say, when documents,
stiff with history, go right into the council chambers
and are rolled up to shake under noses, are constantly read from,
or pounded on, or passed around, the parchment limbers;
and, still later, if these old papers are still being shuffled,
commas will be missing, ashes will disfigure a word;
finally thumbprints will grease out whole phrases, the clear prose
won't mean much; it can never be wholly restored.
Curators mourn the perfect idea, for it crippled
outside of its case. Announce that at least it can move
in the imperfect action, beyond the windy oratory,
of marriage, which is the politics of love.

A Time of Bees

1 9 6 4

Elementary Attitudes

I EARTH

All spring the birds walked on this wormy world.
Now they avoid the ground, lining up on limbs
and fences, beaks held open, panting. And behold,
in a romper suit and tap shoes, my neighbor comes

click, click, past the gawking birds to her patio.
A middle-aged woman—they've known her for months, as have I,
coming down the sidewalk in a housedress twice a day
to throw them breadcrumbs and talk over the fence to me

as I weed and plant or write poems in the backyard garden.
Now I am dazzled by the flowers and by my neighbor in rompers.
She says it's hot, so hot, her house is like an oven.
Aren't the flowers bright, she says. They are worse

than bright these days, it seems to me, they are burning,
blazing in red salvia and orange daylilies,
in marigolds, in geraniums—even the petunias are turning
violent. Rose, red, orange, cerise,

yellow flame together and spread over their borders.
The earth and my diligent gardening, what have we done
to my neighbor? Arms wide out, she suddenly flutters
up into the air and comes down, and leaps again,

and clickety-clickety-clickety *rat-a-tat-tat,*
all over her patio she goes in a frenzy of tapdancing.
What new July conflagration is this, and what
would her husband say, who works in a drugstore? In the spring

she admired my jonquils and, later, the peonies calmly,
tossing bread to the birds as she chatted. They grew tamer and tamer.

Now they are squeaking and wheeling away from what they see,
and I am making good resolutions for next summer:

This collaboration with the earth should be done with care.
Even gardens, it seems, can set off explosions, and so
I'll have blue salvia and blue ageratum next year,
pale petunias, more poems, and some plumbago.

II   AIR

My primitive attitude toward the air makes it impossible
to be anything but provincial. I'll never climb Eiffels,
see Noh plays, big game, leprous beggars, implausible
rites, all in one lifetime. My friends think it's awful.

It leads to overcompensation: in the kitchen, prunes
in the pot roast, kidneys in the wine and the restrained misery
of a hamburger-loving husband; in the yard, prone
plants from far places that never adjusted to Missouri;

in the mind, an unreasoning dislike of haiku, and in least
appropriate gatherings, innocent plans for the remission
of the world's woes—"Well, why don't we all just . . . ?"
People blush for me in political discussion.

It leads also, when visiting friends in California or reading
at the YMHA, to spending three-fourths of the time
on the way and only one-fourth of it there, and to travelling
always in the company of beginners. When I leave home

I ride with farm couples bringing the granddaughter back
for a visit, boys going off to their first big city,
honeymooners, college kids, toddlers who might get airsick,
and Texans who hire a whole car to get drunk cross-country.

Sooner or later most of these graduate to planes,
while I start out all over again on the ground.
The Texans and I are stuck with our beginnings.
To get a panoramic view of my own hometown

I once took a helicopter ride and found everything unreal—
my house, lost in that vista half a mile under,
and whoever was grieving up there in a glass bubble,
pretending to enjoy the sights and growing blinder and blinder.

I can stand an outside view of myself, but nothing
about a bird's-eye view elevates or animates me in the slightest.
Maybe people who don't like air should just stop breathing.
I breathe, but I tend toward asthma and bronchitis.

III FIRE

When feathers and fur came off, and the skin
bared, then we became open
to all manifestations of fire, to the sun's

inconceivable consummations. And I
was born in the busy-ness of that great day
of heat and light, hunting with my whole body.

The blood boils. "A higher temperature,
by hastening the chemical reactions of the creature,
allows it to live more quickly and more

intensely." Biologists are in favor of burning,
and I too, creature singeing
to certain death in the metabolic blessing,

I too celebrate my fires. In Maine
the treetops came sizzling down and I ran
with chipmunks and foxes. Utterances, mean

or stealthy or rhymed, charged, live,
fall all day on the tindery nerves.
These ignitions, and those in the stove

of my flesh, underhand, and speculations,
and barbecue and fireplace in their seasons
keep me quick. Cigarettes blazon

me to words, and bourbon. Some eyes
are best sparks. Our stuff multiplies
in warmth, we are lovers from the first ceremonies

of protein, the lonesome cold stars
miss us. A first breath, and our natures
are afire, we run in the blistering years.

IV WATER

It is hard to remember what one is mostly made of.
Floating on top, as ark, is a sort of sieve
carrying my wet brain, and under the waves
ovaries and liver and other items sway
like the bulbs and stems of some aquatic lily.

But even here, at the confluence of the Missouri
and the Mississippi, late summers are dry
and there is little snow in winter. Abstractions are the key
to being. Scientists flourish, but swimmers
are bitten to death by catfish in these rivers.

When I landed, out of the broken bag of my mother,
heat and buoyancy had to be learned all over,
but there are few such dangerous floods, so far.
On humid days, under a green sea of oak leaves,
I move secretly, like a skin-diver, but don't dive.

The mind is seldom wholly immersed. We live
willingly, fear both drought and drowning, conceive
in swampy places, and drink to provoke love.
When love's unkindness punctures the eyeball, tears
remind us again that we are made of water.

Recovery

I THE DORMITORY

In Mexico the little mixed herds come home in the evening,
slow through that hard-colored landscape, all driven together—
the hens, a few pigs, a burro, two cows, and the thin
perro that is everywhere. It is the same scene here.

The nurses herd us. In our snouts and feathers
we move through the rigid cactus shapes of chairs
colored to lie, belie terror and worse.
Assorted and unlikely as the lives we bear,

we go together to bed, one dozen of us.
It was a hard day's grazing, we fed on spines of courtesy
and scratched up a few dry bugs of kindness.
But we deserved less than that generosity.

Our teats of giving hang dry. Our poor peons are bewildered
and poorer still, the whole landscape is impoverished
by the unnatural economy of this group's greed,
whose bark is bitter, who are swaybacked, fruitless, unfleshed.

The pen echoes to a meaningless moo, "I want to go home,"
one cackles over sins, one yaps in rhythmic complaining,
but those shapes under the sheets are not like mine.
We are locked in unlove. I am sick of my own braying.

The metaphor shakes like my hand. Come, Prince of Pills,
electric kiss, undo us, and we will appear
wearing each other's pain like silk, the awful
richness of feeling we blame, but barely remember.

II THE DOCTORS

Those who come from outside are truly foreign.
How are we to believe in the clear-eyed and clean-shaven?
The jungle I crawl through on my hands and knees,
the whole monstrous ferny land of my own nerves,
hisses and quakes at these upright missionaries
wearing immaculate coats, and will not open.

Mine is waiting outside like a mild boy.
He is unarmed, he will never make it to this anarchy.
Somewhere down his civil streams, through his system,
a survivor came babbling, half-wild from stink and sun,
and news leaked out about our savage customs.
I bit my bloody heart again today.

At night I dream of tables and chairs, beds,
hospitals. I wake. I am up to my waist in mud.
Everything shrieks, cloudbursts of confusion are beating
on my head as I twist and grab for vines, sweating
to make a raft, to tie something together. He is waiting.
I want his words after all, those cheap beads.

Stranger, forgive me, I have clawed as close as I can.
Your trinkets clink to the ground, it is all dark
on the other side of my impenetrable network.
I will wallow and gnaw—but wait, you are coming back,
and at touch, flamethrower, underbrush goes down.
Now I can stand by you, fellow-citizen.

III A MEMORY

"Write a letter to Grandpa," my mother said, but he smelled old.
"He'll give you something nice," she said, but I was afraid.

He never looked at me, he muttered to himself, and he hid
bad things to drink all over his house, and Grandma cried.
A gray stranger with a yellowed mustache, why should I have mailed
my very first message to him? Well, consider the innocent need
that harries us all: "Your Aunt Callie thinks she's smart, but *her* kid
never sent her first letter to Pa." (To hold her I had to be good.)
"You've learned to write. Write Grandpa!" she said, so I did.

It was hard work. "Dear Grandpa, How are you, I am fine,"
but I couldn't come to the end of a word when I came to the margin,
and the lines weren't straight on the page. I erased that paper so thin
you could almost see through it in spots. I couldn't seem to learn
to look ahead. (Mother, remember we both had to win.)
"We are coming to visit you next Sunday if it does not rain.
Yours truly, your loving granddaughter, Mona Van Duyn."
That Sunday he took me aside and gave me the biggest coin
I ever had, and I ran away from the old man.

"Look, Mother, what Grandpa gave me. And as soon as I get
        back home
I'll write him again for another half dollar." But Mother said "Shame!"
and so I was ashamed. But I think at that stage of the game,
or any stage of the game, things are almost what they seem
and the exchange was fair. Later in the afternoon I caught him.
"Medicine," he said, but he must have known his chances were slim.
People don't hide behind the big fern, I wasn't dumb,
and I was Grandma's girl. "So, *Liebling,* don't tell them,"
he said, but that sneaky smile called me by my real name.

Complicity I understood. What human twig isn't bent
by the hidden weight of its wish for some strict covenant?
"Are you going to tell?" he wanted to know, and I said, "No, I won't."
He looked right at me and straightened his mouth and said, "So, *Kind,*
we fool them yet," and it seemed to me I knew what he meant.
Then he reached in his pocket and pulled out two candies covered
        with lint,

and we stood there and each sucked one. *"Ja,* us two, we know what
    we want."
When he leaned down to chuck my chin I caught my first
    Grandpa-scent.
Oh, it was a sweet seduction on pillows of peppermint!
And now, in the middle of life, I'd like to learn how to forgive
the heart's grandpa, mother and kid, the hard ways we have to love.

IV BY THE POND IN THE PARK, BY THE HOSPITAL

The grass is green, the trees and the bench are green.
Parked cars, like aquarium pebbles, circle the pond.
A roar, a dry sprinkle, and a good machine
goes by, cutting grass in a ten-foot strip. In the wind
walk blackbirds. This is the closest I've ever been
to an elegant, high-stepping one. He is watching my hand
and I, watching his red and yellow wing, am sane.

Little dandy, your chemistry, and not your fine
feather, dazzles my half-familiar head,
for, three blocks back, marvelous returns are routine
and the simple map to decay unreadable, or unread.
—To trust perception again is like learning to lean
on water. The water, moving over minnows, is haunted.
Dandelions bloom, the trees and the grass are green.

In the hospital, other matters go on, the obscene
writhing of feelings like worms on hooks, and all mute,
all smelling of wild loss; and now the mowing man
stops and dismounts, throws something in the pond, something light,
then starts up his motors—an empty coffee tin
that scares the minnows away, sinking in the rot
of leaves, to the bottom. That inundation was a dream.

All around the pond a bracelet of cars is curled
and the wind smells green through the mower's unerring noise.
I think through my senses, I chew grass, and a squirrel
chews too, but something hard. Melodrama never has
real answers. Memory will come, like some quiet girl,
slow-spoken and friendly, to tell me whatever it was
I knew I wanted in this grassy world.

Pot-au-Feu

Everything that is going on in Nature ... increase[s] the entropy of the part of the world where it is going on. A living organism ... tends to approach the state of maximum entropy, which is death. It is continually sucking orderliness from its environment [and] freeing itself from all the entropy it cannot help producing ... [and] thus it evades the decay to thermodynamical equilibrium.

SCHRÖDINGER, What Is Life?

I remembered how Mrs. Procter once said to me that, having had a long life of many troubles, sufferings, encumbrances and devastations, it was, in the evening of that life, a singular pleasure, a deeply felt luxury, to her, to sit and read a book: the mere sense of the security of it, the sense that, with all she had outlived, nothing could now happen, *was so great within her.*

HENRY JAMES, Notebooks

It is all too clear that order wasn't our invention.
What we thought we imposed on Nature was her own intention,
and if anyone doubts it, let's see who's the steady old hand
at doting arrangement, her metabolism or our mind:
Watch her anticipate our cellular howl
by spooning out stable linkings of chemical gruel,
or, using the disorder that is death to us,
producing more anchovies and asparagus,
or, for our snacks, slicing up without pause or limit
a million billion other lives a minute.

But, lo, in the high society of consciousness,
we diet to death on our own affectional fuss,
rocking the environment through disordering lips
with the erratic heat motion of our relationships,
turning living to losing, burning with need for our fellow
and filling the air with exhaust for him to swallow;
for to feed on trouble and void a composed overhaul

31

takes a structure humbler than man's, and more Natural.
Yet since mind and body are under each other's thumb
and you come to my mind, something really ought to be done.

You'll have to admit, my darling, that we tire each other,
exhaling such smogs of entropy that the weather
is unwholesome here for us in our weakened condition.
Already we're worn from testing an important mutation
of the internal scene, and we've used lots of heat to start
taking off on those dizzying quantum jumps of the heart,
yet we're forced to keep on regenerating the nicks
of a thousand daily empathic enzyme kicks,
and to carry, wherever we go in our hungry waning,
the sweet encumbrance of one another's meaning.

And so, to balance the emotional wear-and-tear,
let me set a table in the atmosphere.
They say if a glassful of marked molecules were poured
in the Seven Seas, and diligently stirred,
then in any glassful dipped from any ocean
you'd find one hundred out of the original potion.
I can't prove a poem's caloric count is so high,
nor know my particular measuring will reach your eye,
but I'll pour by faith, and believe that wherever you sup
the nourishing orderliness has been thickened up.

The move is mine, my sex is less prone to the torment
of organic dignity, and more attached to our ferment.
I'll debase my system, I'll eat like a weed, and exchange
sounds that I've simmered down to predictable range,
a feast of patterning, a treat of tended lines,
and visible forms, toothsome as tenderloins,
to keep you, sucking the images that bring
you close to receive this artful cherishing,
an inexhaustible fountain of passionate waste
while I grow and blossom on its deathy taste.

POSTSCRIPT:

Watch out, Mrs. Procter, you'll be warmed against your will!
All that jiggling, perverse and thermodynamical,
may suddenly start up again, those turning pages
may tip you right out into life's economic outrages—
and you who have grown so gentle and groomed and tidy
there on the settee, a thoroughly astonished lady
of equilibristic luxury, with a paper plaything,
will burst into metabolic huckstering
and steam back, stoked up on innocent-seeming print,
into devastations, into love's dishevelment.

Notes from a Suburban Heart

> *Freud says that ideas are libidinal cathexes, that is to say, acts of love.*
>
> NORMAN O. BROWN

It's time to put fertilizer on the grass again.
The last time I bought it, the stuff was smelly and black,
and said "made from Philadelphia sewage" on the sack.
It's true that the grass shot up in a violent green,
but my grass-roots patriotism tells me to stick
to St. Louis sewage, and if the Mississippi isn't thick
enough to put in a bag and spread on a lawn,
I'll sprinkle 5-10-5 from nobody's home,
that is to say . . .

it's been a long winter. The new feeder scared off the birds
for the first month it was up. Those stupid starvelings,
puffed up like popcorn against the cold, thought the thing
was a death-trap. The seeds and suet on its boards
go down their gullets now, and come out song,
but scot-free bugs slit up the garden. It is spring.
I've "made bums out of the birdies," in my next-door neighbor's words,
that is to say . . .

your life is as much a mystery to me as ever.
The dog pretends to bite fleas out of sheer boredom,
and not even the daffodils know if it's safe to come
up for air in this crazy, hot-and-cold weather.
Recognitions are shy, the faintest tint of skin
that says we are opening up, is it the same
as it was last year? Who can remember that either?
That is to say,

I love you, in my dim-witted way.

Quebec Suite

for Robert Wykes, Composer

I

Every evening
in this old valley
a bird, a little brown bird,
says thanks
like a sleepy hen
for red
berries.

II

The farmer sits in the sun
and sends nine kids out to work in all directions.
The baby sits on his lap, the toddler leans on his knee.
We have to buy some fishing worms, *les vers.*
"Vingt-cinq vers, s'il vous plaît."
A tow-head boy runs for the can of worms. *"Fait chaud aujourd'hui."*
How pleasant it is.
The sun shines on the thin farm.
The lazy farmer beams at his busy children.
We make the dog howl for the baby.
"Ecoute," the farmer tells his child,
"il parle.
Ecoute,
il parle."

III

The dog changes
here in the open, in wild country.

He wanders with chipmunks,
he saw a moose,
birds beset him,
the skunk under the cabin makes his hair go up.
He spreads his toes to walk the dock
over gaps in the boards
and looks at the lake with calculation.
He is another animal.

IV

I am afraid to swim in this water,
it is so thick with life.
One stranger after another
comes out of it. Right by the boat
there rose at dusk the otter,
dark and slick, as if covered with ointment.
I said, "My God, an alligator!"
And the pike comes up, his vacant golden eye
staring away from the hook.
Perhaps there are eels down under,
looking up at the skating bugs.
In Quebec there is no alligator,
but I see many a stranger.

V

The rocky beaches
are covered with blueberries.
I thought they were blue flowers at first.
Now we use them in pie and pancake,
but still they look like flowers.
Hazy blue,
their smoke rubs off with one touch of the finger.
Under that smear

a deeper blue appears,
as rich and dark as anything we earn.
And so this country feeds our hungers.

VI

The loon is yodeling.
My favorite waterfowl, sleek and swarthy,
a master duck,
he will swim under half the lake
before he comes up with his catch, flapping and swallowing.
But strong as he is, brave as he is,
he is a lonesome bird.
He and his mate must touch each other
all day long across the water
with their cries:
"Here. Here I am. And you? You?"
"Yes, I am here. And you? You? You? You? You?"

Earth Tremors Felt in Missouri

The quake last night was nothing personal,
you told me this morning. I think one always wonders,
unless, of course, something is visible: tremors
that take us, private and willy-nilly, are usual.

But the earth said last night that what I feel,
you feel; what secretly moves you, moves me.
One small, sensuous catastrophe
makes inklings letters, spelled in a worldly tremble.

The earth, with others on it, turns in its course
as we turn toward each other, less than ourselves, gross,
mindless, more than we were. Pebbles, we swell
to planets, nearing the universal roll,
in our conceit even comprehending the sun,
whose bright ordeal leaves cool men woebegone.

A Garland for Christopher Smart

I

For the flower glorifies God and the root parries the adversary. For the right names of flowers are yet in heaven. God make gardners better Nomenclators.

For cosmos, which has too much to live up to,
for hyacinth, which stands for all the accidents of love,
for sunflower, whose leanings we can well understand, for foxglove
and buttercup and snapdragon and candytuft and rue,

and for baby's breath, whose pre-Freudian white we value,
and for daisy, whose little sun confronts the big one
without despair, we thank good gardeners who pun
with eye and heart, who wind the great corkscrew

of naming into the cork on what we know.
While the root parries the adversary, the rest
nuzzles upward through pressure to openness,
and grows toward its name and toward its brightness and sorrow.

And we pray to be better nomenclators, at home
and in field, for the sake of the eye and heart and the claim
of all who come up without their right names,
of all that comes up without its right name.

II

For I bless God for the Postmaster General and all conveyancers of letters under his care especially Allen and Shelvock.

Pastor of these paper multitudes,
the white flocks of our thought that run back and forth,
preserve the coming and going of each nickel's worth
that grazed on the slope of the brain or trotted from its inroad.

39

And all proxies who step to the door in the stead of the upper
left hand corner, keep coming to every house,
that even the most feeble narration may find its use
when it falls into the final slot of the eye, that the mapper

of human dimension may distend that globe each day
and draw each day the connecting network of lines
that greetings and soapflake coupons and valentines
make between one heart and another. We pray

especially for the postman with a built-up shoe who likes dogs
and the one at the parcel post window who bears with good grace
the stupid questions of ladies, and we especially bless
the back under every pack, and the hands, and the legs.

III

> *Let Huldah bless with the Silkworm—the ornaments of the*
> *Proud are from the Bowells of their Betters.*

It was a proud doorway where we saw the spider drop
and swing to drop and swing his silk, the whole
spider rose to raise it, to lower it, fell,
and dangled to make that work out of his drip.

Not speculation, but art. Likewise the honeypot
that makes a fine table, an ornament to bread.
The bees danced out its plot, and feed our pride,
and milked themselves of it, and make us sweet.

And long library shelves make proud homes.
One line, a day in Bedlam, one book, a life
sometimes, sweated onto paper. What king is half
so high as he who owns ten thousand poems?

And the world is lifted up with even more humble words,
snail-scum and limey droppings and fly-blow

and gold loops that dogs have wetted on snow—
all coming and going of beasts and bugs and birds.

     I V

> *Let Jamen rejoice with the bittern blessed be the name of Jesus*
> *for Denver Sluice, Ruston, and the draining of the fens.*

And let any system of sewage that prospers say,
"I am guide and keeper of the human mess,
signature in offal of who, over the face
of the great globe, moves, and is the great globe's glory."

And any long paving, let it utter aloud,
"I bear the coming together and the going apart
of one whose spirit-and-dirt my spirit-and-dirt
eases in passage, for the earth cherishes his load."

Let drainage ditches praise themselves, let them shout,
"I serve his needs for damp and dryness." Let mansions
cry, "We extend his name with our extensions,"
and let prefabricated houses bruit

their mounting up in a moment to preserve this creature.
Let the great globe, which rolls in the only right air,
say, "He delves me and heaps me, he shapes without fear,
he has me in his care, let him take care."

     V

> *For he purrs in thankfulness when God tells him he's a good*
> *cat. For the divine spirit comes about his body to sustain it in*
> *compleat cat. For he camels his back to bear the first notion of*
> *business.*

But let those who invest themselves in the dumb beast
go bankrupt gladly at the end of this investment,

for in answering dumb needs he is most eloquent,
but in sickness cannot ask help, and is often lost.

His smell reaches heaven, hope and faith are his fragrance.
Whether he camels his back or barks, he wears our harness,
he sits under our hearts through all his days, questionless.
His tail directs orchestras of joy at our presence.

For his nature he shivers his coat to cast off flies.
For his nature he hisses, or milks the cushion with his claws.
But he will follow our leg forever, he will give up his mouse,
he will lift up his witless face to answer our voice.

And when he burnishes our ankles or turns away from his breed
to sit beside ours, it may be that God reaches out of heaven
and pets him and tells him he's good, for love has been given.
We live a long time, and God knows it is love we need.

The Gardener to His God

*Amazing research proves simple prayer makes flowers grow
many times faster, stronger, larger.*
                              Advertisement in The Flower Grower

I pray that the great world's flowering stay as it is,
that larkspur and snapdragon keep to their ordinary size,
and bleedingheart hang in its old way, and Judas tree
stand well below oak, and old oaks color the fall sky.
For the myrtle to keep underfoot, and no rose
to send up a swollen face, I pray simply.

There is no disorder but the heart's. But if love goes leaking
outward, if shrubs take up its monstrous stalking,
all greenery is spurred, the snapping lips are overgrown,
and over oaks red hearts hang like the sun.
Deliver us from its giant gardening, from walking
all over the earth with no rest from its disproportion.

Let all flowers turn to stone before ever they begin to share
love's spaciousness, and faster, stronger, larger
grow from a sweet thought, before any daisy
turns, under love's gibberellic wish, to the day's eye.
Let all blooms take shape from cold laws, down from a cold air
let come their small grace or measurable majesty.

For in every place but love the imagination lies
in its limits. Even poems draw back from images
of that one country, on top of whose lunatic stemming
whoever finds himself there must sway and cling
until the high cold God takes pity, and it all dies
down, down into the great world's flowering.

43

Sestina for Warm Seasons

It has been estimated that every seven years or so the body negotiates a complete turnover of all its substance. In other words, your body does not contain a single one of the molecules that were "you" seven years ago.

JOHN PFEIFFER, The Human Brain

Mercy on us for our many birthdays.
Never again can we envy the lobster for his new room
after the molt, nor any grub his changes.
There is no water in the waterfall
that fell before. Out of the familiar face
a stranger comes to stare every seven years.

But he learns to look like us, we browbeat the years
to repeat, to repeat, and so we waste our birthdays.
Even the astronaut, whose rubber face
slews out of shape as he bursts from the old room,
prays to the wires to hold him and let him fall
back home again, braced against all his changes.

Whoever believes the mirrored world, short-changes
the world. Over and over again our years
let us reconsider, make the old molecules fall
from out of our skins, make us go burning with birthdays.
Inside us, the bombardier may shift in his room
ten times, and may, in the instant his murderous face

peels off to show no murderer there, about-face.
And the earth will say his name each time he changes
his name in mid-air, he keeps its living room
open to the coming and going of more years
and of more children who believe in their birthdays.
His missiles mould away and will not fall.

But we were born to love the waterfall
and not the water. By the reflected face
we know each other, never by our birthdays.
Hearts, like lobsters, hide and heal their changes,
for our first self wants itself, and teaches the years
that leak and fill, to reproduce that room.

Even the swollen heart can only make room
for one more self. Dreaming Spring from its Fall,
knee to knee, two sit there and say that years
are all outside, that such absolute face-to-face
stops the spinning story that tells of changes.
And so, my dear, I am afraid of your birthdays.

For love is against birthdays, and locks its room
of mirrors. If your heart changes it will let fall
my face, to roll away in the defacing years.

Open Letter, Personal

Dear Mommy. I do not like you any more. You do not like my
friends so I do not like you. I will be away for some months.
Love, Carla.

                    Note found in the room of an eight-year-old

My friends: If thirty people gather in a room
there is no need for winter heating. For ten years
I have shared your B.T.U.'s, and I think at the same time
of all the summer evenings when fans and airconditioners
were helpless against our being together and our smoke would burn
each other's eyes raw. We are both better and worse
since we met. Better and worse to be warm than lonesome.

Last spring the young writer came again, and we spoke of friends.
But this time he looked at me with his doctor's eyes in his head,
hooded and light like a river turtle's, and talked of their wounds
and drives and systems of aggression, hostility and need,
until I saw them, the skeletons of big fish, stand
around him, bleached and quiet. I am not that safe, I said,
from the hands of my friends, nor are they that safe at my hands.

It is in the strain, in the reaching of the whole mind to see
what it is that is coming toward us, what we are coming toward,
as the earliest essays on Wallace Stevens' poetry
touch and retouch the lines, trying to tell, but the words
are just behind the tip of the tongue—it is there, below
knowledge, before the settled image, that the lovely, hard
poem or person is befriended. Friendship is that sweaty play.

But believe me, my friends, we are in the late essays. A decade
has used us so that when we go out, we are at home.
We know each other's gestures like a book, we can hide
nothing personal but the noises of sex and digestion and boredom,
can leave each other only when we go to bed

or to work—the canvas, the class, the court, the consulting room,
typewriter or lab. I am trying to say our friendship is dead.

Surely the jig is up. We've pinned each other down.
We know which of us will like which new novel, and why,
which of us will flirt, and with whom, and how long it will go on,
which of us are jealous of what in each other, and which fake, or lie,
or don't shave their legs, or don't like cheese, and very soon
your smallest children will tire of naming my couch pillows,
black, white, green, lavender and brown.

And worse: I have seen you betray affection, make a fool
of your mate, and you have seen me. I've watched you cringe and shake
and writhe in your selves, and you have seen me in my hospital.
I have given you paper faces and they have grown lifelike,
and you have stuck on my lips in this sheep's smile.
If I could get free of you I would change, and I would choke
this stooge to death and be proud and violent for a while.

As long as the moon hides half her face we are friends of the moon.
As long as sight reaches through space we are fond of the star.
But there is no space, and what light is yours and what is mine
is impossible to tell in this monstrous Palomar
where each pock is plain. I cannot dry you into fishbone
essences, I have grown into your shape and size and mirror.
I think I see you on the streets of every strange town.

We know the quickest way to hurt each other, and we have
used that knowledge. See, it is here, in the joined strands
of our weaknesses, that we are netted together and heave
together strongly like the great catch of mackerel that ends
an Italian movie. I feel your bodies smell and shove
and shine against me in the mess of the pitching boat. My friends,
we do not like each other any more. We love.

A Time of Bees

Love is never strong enough to find the words befitting it.

CAMUS

All day my husband pounds on the upstairs porch.
Screeches and grunts of wood as the wall is opened
keep the whole house tormented. He is trying to reach
the bees, he is after bees. This is the climax, an end
to two summers of small operations with sprays and ladders.

Last June on the porch floor I found them dead,
a sprinkle of dusty bugs, and next day a still worse
death, until, like falling in love, bee-haunted,
I swept up bigger and bigger loads of some hatch,
I thought, sickened, and sickening me, from what origin?

My life centered on bees, all floors were suspect. The search
was hopeless. Windows were shut. I never find
where anything comes from. But in June my husband's fierce
sallies began, inspections, cracks located
and sealed, insecticides shot; outside, the bees' course

watched, charted; books on bees read.
I tell you I swept up bodies every day on the porch.
Then they'd stop, the problem was solved; then they were there again,
as the feelings make themselves known again, as they beseech
sleepers who live innocently in will and mind.

It is no surprise to those who walk with their tigers
that the bees were back, no surprise to me. But they had
left themselves so lackluster, their black and gold furs
so deathly faded. Gray bugs that the broom hunted
were like a thousand little stops when some great lurch

of heart takes place, or a great shift of season.
November it came to an end. No bees. And I could watch

48

the floor, clean and cool, and, from windows, the cold land.
But this spring the thing began again, and his curse
went upstairs again, and his tinkering and reasoning and pride.

It is the man who takes hold. I lived from bees, but his force
went out after bees and found them in the wall where they hid.
And now in July he is tearing out the wall, and each
board ripped brings them closer to his hunting hand.
It is quiet, has been quiet for a while. He calls me, and I march

from a dream of bees to see them, winged and unwinged,
such a mess of interrupted life dumped on newspapers
dirty clots of grubs, sawdust, stuck fliers, all smeared
together with old honey, they writhe, some of them, but who cares?
They go to the garbage, it is over, everything has been said.

But there is more. Wouldn't you think the bees had suffered
enough? This evening we go to a party, the breeze
dies, late, we are sticky in our old friendships and light-headed.
We tell our funny story about the bees.
At two in the morning we come home, and a friend,

a scientist, comes with us, in his car. We're going to save
the idea of the thing, a hundred bees, if we can find
so many unrotted, still warm but harmless, and leave
the rest. We hope that the neighbors are safe in bed,
taking no note of these private catastrophes.

He wants an enzyme in the flight-wing muscle. Not a bad
thing to look into. In the night we rattle and raise
the lid of the garbage can. Flashlights in hand,
we open newspapers, and the men reach in a salve
of happenings. I can't touch it. I hate the self-examined

who've killed the self. The dead are darker, but the others have
moved in the ooze toward the next moment. My God
one half-worm gets its wings right before our eyes.

49

Searching fingers sort and lay bare, they need
the idea of bees—and yet, under their touch, the craze

for life gets stronger in the squirming, whitish kind.
The men do it. Making a claim on the future, as love
makes a claim on the future, grasping. And I, underhand,
I feel it start, a terrible, lifelong heave
taking direction. Unpleading, the men prod

till all that grubby softness wants to give, *to give.*

An Annual and Perennial Problem

> *Among annuals and perennials, there are not many that can*
> *properly be classed among these* Heavy *and frankly seductive*
> *odors. No gardener should plant these in quantities near the*
> *house, or porch, or patio without realizing that many of them,*
> *in spite of exquisite fragrance, have a past steeped in sin.*
> Taylor's Garden Guide

One should have known, I suppose, that you can't even trust
the lily-of-the-valley, for all it seems so chaste.

The whole lily family, in fact, is "brooding and sultry."
It's a good thing there's a Garden Guide, nothing paltry

about *their* past. Why, some are so "stinking" one expert cried,
" 'may dogs devour its hateful bulbs!' " Enough said.

We'd better not try to imagine . . . But it's hard to endure
the thought of them sitting brazenly in churches, looking pure.

The tuberose fragrance "is enhanced by dusk and becomes"
(remember, they're taken right into some people's homes,

perhaps with teenage children around in that air!)
"intoxicating with darkness." Well, there you are.

You hear it said sometimes that in a few cases
the past can be lived down. There's no basis

for that belief—these flowers have had plenty of time.
Sinners just try to make decent folks do the same.

What we've always suspected is true. We're not safe anywhere.
Dark patios, of course—but even at our own back door

from half a block off the jasmine may try to pollute us,
and Heaven protect us all from the trailing arbutus!

To See, To Take

1970

A Christmas Card, after the Assassinations

What is to be born already fidgets in the stem,
near where the old leaves loosened, resembling them,
or burns in the cell, ready to be blue-eyed,
or, in the gassy heavens, gathers toward a solid,
except for that baby mutant, Christ or beast,
who forms himself from a wish, our best or last.

Causes

Questioned about why she had beaten her spastic child to death, the mother told police, "I hit him because he kept falling off his crutches."

News item

Because one's husband is different from one's self,
the pilot's last words were "Help, my God, I'm shot!"
Because the tip growth on a pine looks like Christmas tree candles,
cracks appear in the plaster of old houses.

And because the man next door likes to play golf,
a war started up in some country where it is hot,
and whenever a maid waits at the bus-stop with her bundles,
the fear of death comes over us in vacant places.

It is all foreseen in the glassy eye on the shelf,
woven in the web of notes that sprays from a trumpet,
announced by a salvo of crackles when the fire kindles,
printed on the nature of things when a skin bruises.

And there's never enough surprise at the killer in the self,
nor enough difference between the shooter and the shot,
nor enough melting down of stubs to make new candles
as the earth rolls over, inverting billions of houses.

Leda

Did she put on his knowledge with his power
Before the indifferent beak could let her drop?

Not even for a moment. He knew, for one thing, what he was.
When he saw the swan in her eyes he could let her drop.
In the first look of love men find their great disguise,
and collecting these rare pictures of himself was his life.

Her body became the consequence of his juice,
while her mind closed on a bird and went to sleep.
Later, with the children in school, she opened her eyes
and saw her own openness, and felt relief.

In men's stories her life ended with his loss.
She stiffened under the storm of his wings to a glassy shape,
stricken and mysterious and immortal. But the fact is,
she was not, for such an ending, abstract enough.

She tried for a while to understand what it was
that had happened, and then decided to let it drop.
She married a smaller man with a beaky nose,
and melted away in the storm of everyday life.

The Creation

Now that I know you are gone
I have to try, like Rauschenberg,
to rub out, line by line,
your picture, feeling as I rub
the maker's most inhuman
joy, seeing as I rub
the paper's slow, awful return
to possibility.
Five times you screamed and won
from your short body a big boy
or a tall girl to join
the rest of us here,
and now let daughter or son
wear all that's left of your face
when this drawing's undone.

It is hard, heavy work.
The pencil indented the grain
of the paper, and I scour
a long time on a cheekbone
that doesn't want to disappear,
hoping my fingers won't learn
its line from going over and over
it. I replace your chin
with dead white.
Once, in a little vain
coquettishness, you joined
your party late, hair down
to your waist, and let the men
watch you twist it around
to a blonde rope and pin
the richness of its coils
into a familiar bun.
And now I make you bald

with my abrasion.
The hours we had to drink
before you'd put the dinner on!
My eraser's wet with sweat
as it moves on a frown
of long, tipsy decision:
were we all so drunk
it didn't matter, or should you strain
the Mornay sauce?
Already we are worn,
the eraser and I, and we
are nearing your eyes. Your garden
was what you saw each morning,
and your neighbor's, making fun
of her oversolicitude:
"I swear that woman
digs her plants up every day
to see if their roots have grown."
You tucked the ticklish roots
of half-grown youngsters, back in
and pressed the tilth around them.
Your eyes were an intervention.
You saw your words begin
a moody march to the page
when you tried to write what you'd seen
in poems you brought out one by one
to show us, getting braver
slowly—yes, too slowly. When
you finally sent some off—
too slowly—a magazine
took one and printed it
too slowly; you had just gone.
If I raise my head from this work
what I see is that the sun
is shining anyway,
and will continue to shine
no matter whose pale Dutch blue

eyes are closed or open,
no matter what graphite memories
do or do not remain,
so I erase and don't
look up again.
When I answer the phone
I don't any longer expect
your jerky conversation—
one funny little comment,
then silence until I began
trying to fill it myself;
at last the intention
would appear, "Come for dinner
and help me entertain
someone I'm scared of." It was hard
to believe you were often
really sick and afraid.
You heard the tune
of our feelings, I think,
over the phone, even.
You liked a joke.
You loved Beethoven.
And this is the end of your ear.
I see your nose redden
with summer allergies,
wrinkle at your husband's pun
and then straighten and fade.
What is left of you is graven,
almost, into one kind of smile.
I don't think I can mourn
much more than I already have
for this loved irritant—prune
pucker, with ends of lips
pulled up. More than your grin
it lasts, and with it lasts
a whole characterization
I can't dispose of

unless I rub clear through and ruin
this piece of anti-art.
When our repartee would run
too fast, or someone's anecdote
run long, or someone mention
a book you hadn't read,
that smile meant you were hidden.
It meant you needed time
to think of something clever or mean,
or that you thought we'd gone too far
from the gentle and sane.
It meant you were our wise,
dear, vulnerable, human
friend, as true and false as life
would let you be, and when
I move you that much farther from
your self to generalization
there is a blur
and your smile stops. This thing is done.

Swept empty by a cyclone
inside, I lift the paper.
But before I blow it clean,
sketched now in rubber crumbs,
another face is on it—mine,
Sneak, Poet, Mon-
ster,
trying to rob you with words.

Your death was your own.

The Pietà, Rhenish, 14th C., the Cloisters

He stares upward at a monstrous face,
as broad as his chest, as long as he is
from the top of his head to his heart. All her
feeling and fleshiness is there.

To be on her lap is to be all shrunken
to a little composition of bone
and held away from her upper body,
which, like an upended cot smoothed neatly

and topped with a tight, girlish bolster
of breasts, rises behind him, queer
to them both, as if no one had ever rested
upon it, or rumpled it, or pressed it.

And so it stands free of suffering.
But above it, the neck, round and wrinkling
from the downward tilt of the head it's bearing,
bears the full weight of that big thing.

It is a face that, if he could see
as we are forced to see, and if he
knew, as we cannot help but know, that
his dead, dangling, featureless, granite

feet would again have to touch the ground,
would make him go mad, would make his hand,
whose hard palm is the same size
as one of his mother's tearless eyes,

hit it, since nothing in life can cure
pain of this proportion. To see her
is to understand that into the blast
of his agony she turned, full-faced,

and the face began to melt and ache,
the brows running down from their high arc
to the cheekbone, the features falling toward the chin,
leaving the huge forehead unlined, open,

until, having felt all it could feel,
her face numbed and began to congeal
into this. With horror he'd have to see
the massive girl there, vapidly

gazing, stupid, stupefied.
If he said, "Willingly I dried
out of consciousness and turned to the slight
husk you hold on your knee, but let

an innocent, smaller love of a son
hold me, let not my first stone
be the heart of this great, grotesque mother.
Oh God, look what we've done to each other,"

then from the head her slow wit,
stirring, would speak, "My darling, it was not
I who belittled you, but love
itself, whose nature you came to believe

was pure possibility, though you came through
its bloody straits. And not you,
but love itself, has made me swell
above you, gross and virginal

at once. I touch what's left on my knee
with the tips of my fingers—it is an ugly,
cold corrugation. Here on my lap,
close in my arms, I wanted to keep

both the handsome, male load of your whole
body and the insupportable,

complete weightlessness of your loss.
The holy and incestuous

met and merged in my love, and meet
in every love, and love is great.
But unmanned spirit or unfleshed man
I cannot cradle. Child, no one can."

Advice to a God

Before you leave her, the woman who thought you lavish,
whose body you led to parade without a blush
the touching vulgarity of the *nouveau-riche,*

whose every register your sexual coin
crammed full, whose ignorant bush mistook for sunshine
the cold, brazen battering of your rain,

rising, so little spent, strange millionaire
who feels in his loins' pocket clouds of power
gathering again for shower upon golden shower,

say to her, since she loves you, "Those as unworldly
as you are fated, and I can afford, to be
may find in Love's bed the perfect economy,

but, in all of his other places, a populace
living in fear of his management, his excess
of stingy might and extravagant helplessness.

Turn from him, Danae. I am greater by far,
whose flower reseeds without love for another flower,
whose seas part without loneliness, whose air

brightens or darkens heartlessly. By chance
I have come to you, and a progeny of events,
all that the mind of man calls consequence,

will follow my coming, slaughter and marriage, intrigue,
enchantment, definition of beauty, hag
and hero, a teeming, throwaway catalogue

of the tiniest, riskiest portion of my investment.
Yet pity your great landlord, for if I lent
so much as an ear to you, one loving tenant,

your bankrupt scream as I leave might tempt me to see
all creation in the ungainly, ungodly
throes of your individuality."

Billings and Cooings from the Berkeley Barb (Want-Ad Section)

. . . Couples sought (enclose photograph please)
by couple who've expeditiously run through
(and are eager for permutations *à quatre, à seize*)
all known modes of the sweet conjunction for two.

Gay guy needs, for a few conventional
dances and such, fem Lez to pose as date,
in return for which she can really have a ball
with her butch friend at parties he'll give in private.

How bright the scholars who use a previous schooling
to get the further enlightenment they want!
Well-rounded girl will do it hung from the ceiling
by ropes in exchange for a used copy of Kant.

A youth who pines in his present incarnation
but remembers with pleasure being a parakeet
seeks a girl just as reluctantly human
and formerly budgerigar, for a mate.

At Blank's bar, woman who'd like the *frisson*
of sex with an ex-guru should ask for Gus.
An A.C.-D.C. will share pad with someone
similarly ambidextrous.

Boy seeks cute girlfriend to share his sack
How startling now the classic or pastoral!
and lists his qualifications to attract:
"tall, dark, sensitive, handsome, sterile."

Student who can't remember the phone number
or the face of student he met at Jack's last fall,

but can't forget the hard nipples, would like her
to dial xx (transvestites need not call).

Delights they probably never knew they could have
nineteen-year-old will guarantee to disclose
to women between fifty and sixty-five
with unusually big feet or long toes.

How dazzling love's infinite variety!
How fertile is nature in her forms of joy!
Male seeks, in the area around Berkeley,
another male whose fetish is corduroy . . .

Footnotes to The Autobiography of Bertrand Russell

for Viktor

I

*(we did not go to bed the first time we were lovers, as there
was too much to say.)*

Once out of Eden, love learned its deviousness
and found in Word its wiliest metaphor;
so if a heart, untouched and in rich disguise,
using the lips to speak of weather and war,

should receive from another masquerading heart
conversing of war and weather, the news of its need,
both may be tempted by art for the sake of art.
A long-winded discourse no other member can read,

page after page on weather and war, may ensue,
they think, with margins of blank sophistication.
And should the pedantic body scrawl there "How true!"
dumbfounded lovers can continue the conversation.

II

*Her objections to [marrying] him are the following: (a) He
sleeps with 7 dogs on his bed. She couldn't sleep a wink in such
circumstances. (b) . . .*

This seems, in a world where love must take its chances,
undue distaste for the first of its circumstances.

What in so snug a sleeper could be more rare
than to sense in so snuggling a crowd something lacking there?

And it seems that the lady lacks sensitivity
to how brilliant her hymeneal reception might be:

First, on the heated bed he'd push aside
seven drowsing dogs to insert one blushing bride,

and surely all other nuptial welcome pales
before a sweet thrashing given her by seven tails!

Fourteen ears attuned to their master's voice
would attend the orisons of their master's choice

in bitches, and should some Donne-reading flea propose
a speedy union, he'd suffer twenty-eight paws.

Garlanded, guarded, graced with panting devotion,
the human pair would partake of wedded emotion,

she with unwinking eyes on the dogs, and he
jostling dogs with his old impunity

until, under his lips, her eyelids would close
and the dear beast of the heart come to discompose

the bed whereon seven pairs of canine eyes
would gaze at each other with a wild surmise.

Postcards from Cape Split

I

"What is that flower?" we asked right away. What a sight!
From the rocks of the beach all the way up the hill to our house,
and all around the house and on either side of the road,
a solid ocean of flowers, shifting in the wind, shifting
in shades of pink like strokes of a brush. Heliotrope.
Pinky-white masses of bloom on five-foot red stems.
"My father brought it here," our landlady says.
" 'Be careful of heliotrope,' they told him, 'it spreads like a weed.' "
It has taken the hill and the house, it is on its way down the road.
Little paths are scythed through heliotrope to the sea,
from the house to the outhouse, from the road to the house,
and a square of back yard is cut away from the flowers.
"The heliotrope is taking my raspberry patch,"
the neighbor tells us, and, snuggled in heliotrope,
the kitchen gardens fight for their viney lives,
one here, one there. You can't even see them until
you're right on their edge, leaning over the heliotrope.

II

Everything looks like the sea but the sea.
The sea looks like a lake
except when fucus is dumped on its low-tide border
like heaps of khaki laundry left out to rot—
this seems a capacity for waste that is worthy of an ocean.
But the dining room floor looks like the sea,
wide old boards, painted dark green,
that heave and ripple in waves.
Light hits the crest of each board and gives it a whitecap.

The house saves everything,
crutches and children's sleds, painted cups without handles,

chairs without seats, dried sweetgrass, fir tips in pillows.
It must be almost as old as it looks—
the father of our seventy-year-old landlady built it.
It is buffed by the salt winds to elephant color.

One goes on vacation to housekeep another way.
I have made a chart of the tides,
which are now a part of my order for a few weeks.
I have learned the perverse ways of this house—
sink and refrigerator in the kitchen,
stove, dishes, and table in the dining room.
I have tied back white net curtains,
still creased from display in the dimestore.
I have found paths through heliotrope
to each new neighbor.

III

We move in a maze of villages—
Addison, East Addison, South Addison,
Machias, East Machias, and Machiasport.
(The *ch* is pronounced *ch,* and not *k.*)
The lobsters and cheese are at South Addison,
the doctor, the bakery, and the liquor store are at Machias,
the nearest post office and, they say, frozen chicken livers
are at Addison, the seafood cannery is at East Machias.
East Addison and Machiasport we have so far been able to ignore.

The kitchen in this house is papered in villages.
Five villages from floor to ceiling, I don't know how many
across the wall. There is no place to locate one's self.
Still, because the dog snores by the oilstove, the brown
sparrow-size birds squeak cheerily in a spruce by the outhouse,
little toy boats are out on the sea after lobsters, the sun
is warm and the heliotrope is blowing like waves,
because, my God, it *is* pleasant here,

we can surely live uncentered for three weeks,
gleaning a little from one village, a little from another.

    IV

Who would believe that we could learn to cook, drink, bathe,
shave, fill the dog's bowl, the icecube tray, the vase
for wildflowers, and keep ourselves in clean clothes and towels
on two buckets of water a day? Of course we steam mussels
and lobsters in, drive the dog into, wade in, and gaze upon
the sea, and that saves on our freshwater needs.
Each morning we take our two buckets, go down the road
to the landlord's house, walk in the back door
(as we were told to do) and get our water
and a hot donut, or a story about the old times here.
But we want to be self-sufficient the rest of the day,
neither past nor people between us and the ocean,
and so we have learned this new skill for the summer.

But what a small thirst one has, in summer, for the everyday water,
whereas, for the salty stranger, from here to the horizon
at high tide is no more than we can drink in
in a single day.

    V

There are thirty-five stalks of corn in our garden.
Our landlord is trying to raise some corn this year.
He has staked and tied every stalk
to hold it against the sea winds.
Our landlady dopes the tassels with liniment
to keep the raccoons off.
Except for its corn and its heliotrope wall,
our garden is just like others all over the Cape:
four rows of potatoes,

two rows of string beans,
one row each of peas and beets,
one row of squash,
and one row of dahlias.
The man from across the bar
brought us a sea-moss pudding
in a silver dish.

VI

Our landlord's youngest son, the lobsterman,
comes in his lobstering boots, turned halfway down,
to fix our oilstove. I am dazzled by the man in boots.
It is as if a heron stood in my dining room.

His father sits in a rocker by his kitchen stove,
knitting the twine innards for lobster traps
and saying, "When we were young I'd go out in a skiff,
why, right off here, and spear a half bushel of flounder
while She cooked breakfast. We had dried fish all winter,
and they was *some good,* I tell you." The day's light changes.

We drove inland a ways, through the Blueberry Barrens.
Mile after mile, from road to the far mountains,
of furzy wasteland, flat. You almost miss it.
Suddenly, under that empty space, you notice
the curious color of the ground. Blue mile, blue mile,
and then a little bent-over group of Indians
creeping down string-marked aisles. Blue mile, blue mile,
and then more Indians, pushing their forked dustpans.
It looks like a race at some country picnic, but lost
in that monstrous space, under that vacant sky.

Why am I dazzled? It is only another harvest.
The world blooms and we all bend and bring
from ground and sea and mind its handsome harvests.

74

In the Hospital for Tests

My mother's friend cooked for the drunk-and-disorderlies,
and so, when I was ten, I peeked at a cell,
and that's what I'd swear this room came out of—the county jail.
But here in a sweat lies a strange collection of qualities,
with me inside it, or maybe only somewhere near it,
while all the nonsense of life turns serious again—
bowel movements, chickenpox, the date of one's first menstruation,
the number of pillows one sleeps on, postnasal drip—
"It has very high arches," I hear the resident note.
He has worked his way down over its ridges and jerks,
its strings and moistures, coursings, lumps and networks,
to the crinkled and slightly ticklish soles of its feet.
"Don't worry, if there's anything going on here," the interne says,
"we'll find it. I myself have lots of ideas."

Across the room, over a jungle of plants,
blooming, drooping, withering, withered and dead,
a real face watches, freckled and flat blue eyed.
Sometimes her husband visits, a man of plaid shirts
and apologetic smiles, and sometimes three red-head
little girls in stairsteps, too scared to talk out loud.

In twenty-four hours, the hefty nurse, all smiles,
carries out my urine on her hip like a jug of cider,
a happy harvest scene. My roommate, later,
gets on a stretcher, clutching her stomach, and it wheels
her off down the halls for a catheter in her heart.
There's one chance in five hundred she'll die in the test. She'd like
to live for two more years for the children's sake.
Her husband waits in the room. He sweats. We both sweat.

She was only fifteen when they married, he says, but she told him
she was past eighteen and he didn't find out for years.
She's wheeled back, after a feverish two hours,

with black crochet on her arm. She was conscious all the time,
and could feel whatever it was, the little box, go
through her veins to the left of the chest from the right elbow.

The leukemia across the hall, the throat cancer a few doors down,
the leaky valve who has to sleep on eight pillows—
these sit on our beds and talk of the soggy noodles
they gave us for lunch, and the heat, and how long, how soon.
The room stinks of my urine and our greed.
To live, to live at all costs, that's what we want.
We never knew it before, but now we hunt
down the healthy nurses with our eyes. We gobble our food.
Intruders come from outside during visiting hours
and chatter about silly things, no longer our affairs.

"A little more blood, I'm on the trail." He'll go far,
my interne. My roommate gets on the stretcher again;
she comes back almost dead, but they give her oxygen.
She whistles for breath, her face is swollen and sore
and dark. She spits up white rubber. The bronchoscope,
that's what it was this time, and more tests to come.
She wishes her husband had been here after this one.
They were going to do the other lung too, but they had to stop.

In the middle of the night her bed blazes white in the darkness.
Three red-headed daughters dangle from her lightcord.
The nurse holds a cup to her lips. It is absurd,
she is swallowing my poems. The air knots like a fist,
or a heart, the room presses in like a lung. It is empty
of every detail but her life. It is bright and deathly.

"You can go home this afternoon. You're all checked out."
My doctor is grinning over the obscene news.
My roommate sits up and listens. "God only knows
what causes these things, but you've nothing to worry about."
In shame I pack my bag and make my call.

She reads a magazine while I wait for my husband.
She doesn't speak, she is no longer my friend.
We say goodbye to each other. I hope she does well.
In shame I walk past the staring eyes and their reproaches
all down the hall. I walk out on my high arches.

Remedies, Maladies, Reasons

Her voice, that scooped me out of the games of the others
to dump me in bed at seven for twelve years,

and yelled me up to my feet if I sat on the ground,
liable to catch pneumonia, and each year penned

the feet, that wanted to walk bare, or hike
or wade, in the cramping, pygmy shoes of the chronic

invalid, intoned each time I raged or cried
the old story of how I'd nearly died

at six weeks from nursing a serum she'd taken,
so I'd never be well. Each day all over again

she saved me, pitted against rain, shine, cold, heat,
hunting in my mouth each morning for a sore throat,

laying a fever-seeking hand on my forehead
after school, incanting "Did your bowels move good?

Wrap up before you go out and don't play hard.
Are you *sure* you're not coming down with a cold? You look tired,"

keeping me numb on the couch for so many weeks,
if somehow a wily cough, flu, or pox

got through her guard, my legs would shake and tingle,
trying to find the blessed way back to school.

Girl Scouts, green apples, tree climbs, fairs—the same
no. "But the other kids . . ." "Well, you're not like *them*."

Food was what, till I gagged, she kept poking in,
and then, with high enemas, snaked out again;

her one goose, refusing to fatten, I showed
her failure and shamed her with every bone I had.

If I screamed that I'd run away if I couldn't go,
she'd say, "All right, but that'll be the end of you,

you'll get sick and who'll pay the doctor bill?
You'll *die,* you know as well as I do you will."

I was scared to die. I had to carry a hankyful
of big white mineral pills, a new cure-all,

for months, and gulp them in classes every half hour.
They spilled on the floor in front of my favorite teacher.

A spastic went jerking by. "That's how *you'll* get
from twitching your finger all the time. Now quit it!"

A bandaged head moaned in the hospital. "Mastoid.
That's how *you'll* be if you don't stop blowing hard."

Only once, dumbfounded, did she ever notice a thing
that might be thought of as strength in me. Breaking

another free yardstick from the dry-goods store
on a butt and legs still bad, she found her junior

in high school fighting back till we rolled on the floor.
That night she said I wouldn't get spanked anymore.

She took me to college and alerted the school nurse.
I went in without looking back. For four years

I tested each step, afraid to believe it was me
bearing like a strange bubble the health of my body

as I walked the fantastic land of the ordinary
and learned how to tear up the letters, "You *know* how I worry,

for my sake please don't do it . . . don't try it . . . don't go . . .
You *surely* wouldn't want to make me worry like I do!"

Marriage, work, books, years later, called
to help them when she and Dad both lay in bed,

I first stepped back in their house for a stay of more
than a few days. Soon she was crying "Come back here!

Don't you dare go outside that door without your sweater!"
"But it's hot out," said the innocent, visiting neighbor.

"Oh, but she's never been well, I have to keep watching
her like a hawk or she comes right down with something."

There, on my big shoulders, against such proof—
a quarter of a century of the charmed life

I'd been living outside the door—she could still see
the weak, rolling head of a death-threatened baby.

In a hundred visits and fifteen hundred letters
she's been showing herself to me for thirty years

(as well as six thousand days of retrospect)
in clear colors. I know what to expect

before I open my ears or the envelope.
She had to get up three times a night to "dope"

a sore, she "gargled and sprayed" for a week so as not
to get "what was going around." There was blood in the snot

she blew out last month. She "hawks up big gobs
of stuff" that is almost orange. All of her tubes

are blocked. Her face turned purple. Lettuce she ate
was "passed" whole, "green as grass" in the toilet.

She "came within an inch" of a "stoppage," but mineral oil
saved her from all but "a running-off of the bowel."

Sniffing her mucus or sweat or urine, she marvels
anew at how "rotten" or "rank" or "sour" it smells.

There's never been any other interesting news.
Homer of her own heroic course, she rows

through the long disease of living, and celebrates
the "blood-red" throat, the yellow pus that "squirts"

from a swelling, the taste, always "bitter as gall,"
that's "belched up," the bumps that get "sore as a boil,"

the gas that makes her "blow up tight as a drum,"
the "racing heart," the "new kind of bug," the "same

old sinus," the "god-awful cold"—all things that make
her "sick as a dog" or "just a nervous wreck."

Keeping her painstaking charts, first mariner
of such frightful seas, she logs each degree and number.

("Three hundred thousand units of penicillin
he gave me last Thursday!" "I puked four times, and the last one

was *pure bile!*" "Fever way up to ninety-
nine-point-nine!") Daily, but not humbly,

she consults the eight shelves of the six-foot, steel,
crammed-with-medication oracle.

I know what she is, I know what she always was:
a hideous machine that pumps and wheezes,

suppurating, rotting, stinking, swelling,
its valves and pipes shrieking, its fluids oozing

in the open, in violent color, for students to learn
the horror, the nausea, of being human.

And yet, against all the years of vivid, never-
varying evidence, when I look at her

I see an attractive woman. And looking back,
testing the truth of a child's long-ago look,

I still see the mother I wanted, that I called to come,
coming. From the dark she rushes to my bedroom,

switching the lamp on, armed with pills, oils, drops,
gargles, liniments, flannels, salves, syrups,

waterbag, icebag. Bending over me,
giant, ferocious, she drives my Enemy,

in steamy, hot-packed, camphorated nights,
from every sickening place where he hides and waits.

Do you think I don't know how love hallucinates?

Open Letter from a Constant Reader

To all who carve their love on a picnic table
or scratch it on smoked-glass panes of a public toilet,
I send my thanks for each plain and perfect fable
of how the three pains of the body, surfeit,

hunger, and chill (or loneliness), create
a furniture and art of their own easing.
And I bless two public sites and, like Yeats,
two private sites where the body receives its blessing.

Nothing is banal or lowly that tells us how well
the world, whose highways proffer table and toilet
as signs and occasions of comfort for belly and bowel,
can comfort the heart too, somewhere in secret.

Where so much constant news of good has been put,
both fleeting and lasting lines compel belief.
Not by talent or riches or beauty, but
by the world's grace, people have found relief

from the worst pain of the body, loneliness,
and say so with a simple heart as they sit
being relieved of one of the others. I bless
all knowledge of love, all ways of publishing it.

The Miser

I was out last night,
the very picture of a sneak, dark and hunched-over,
breaking and entering again.
Why do I do it?

And why, when I can afford serious residences,
do I keep to this one room?
Perhaps if I had not lost track of the difference
between the real and the ideal
it would never have happened.
I hide here almost entirely now.

When I go out, when I creep into those silent houses,
I steal newspapers.
An armload, no more than I can carry comfortably.
Sometimes they are already tied up
on the side porch or by the kitchen stove.
Nobody misses them.
They think each other or the maid
has carried them out to the street.

They say there is something intractable out there,
the Law, the Right to Privacy,
the World.
In the days when my obsession was only a woundup toy,
squeaking and jabbering in my chest,
I could have believed them.

I sit by the window today
(there is very little space left now,
though I have left corridors wide enough to walk through
so I won't lose touch),
holding my latest on my lap,

handling them, fondling them, taking in every column.
They are becoming more and more precious.

My delusion grows and spreads.
Lately it seems to me
as I read of murders, wars, bankruptcies, jackpot winnings,
the news is written in that perfect style
of someone speaking to the one
who knows and loves him.

Long before they miss me, I think,
the room will be perfectly solid.
When they break in the door and, unsurprised,
hardened to the most bizarre vagaries,
begin to carry out my treasure,
death's what they'll look for underneath it all,
those fluent, muscled, imaginative men,
sweating in their innocent coveralls.

But I will be out in broad daylight by then,
answering,
having accepted utterly the heart's conditions.
Tell them I wish them well, always,
that I've been happy.

Relationships

The legal children of a literary man
remember his ugly words to their mother.
He made them keep quiet and kissed them later.
He made them stop fighting and finish their supper.
His stink in the bathroom sickened their noses.
He left them with sitters in lonesome houses.
He mounted their mother and made them wear braces.
He fattened on fame and raised them thin.

But the secret sons of the same man
spring up like weeds from the seed of his word.
They eat from his hand and it is not hard.
They unravel his sweater and swing from his beard.
They smell in their sleep his ferns and roses.
They hunt the fox on his giant horses.
They slap their mother, repeating his phrases,
and swell in his sight and suck him thin.

The Twins

My sweet-faced, tattletale brother was born blind,
but the colors drip in his head. He paints with his fingers.
All day with his pots and paper he follows me around
wherever I set up my easel, till I pinch his bat ears,

then before he goes he swears he didn't feel anything.
But he knows my feelings, sneaks them out of my skin.
The things he knows! Leaving me squeezed and sulking,
he pretends he felt them himself and tells everyone.

Nobody ever blames him. He's terribly talented.
The world, glimpsing itself through him, will grow
sick with self-love, it seems, and under his eyelid
lie down, in burning shame, with its own shadow,

whereas, on my canvas, it wears its gray and brown
like a fat beaver, and even as I sweat on my brush,
all forms, at its simpleminded toothy grin,
branches, limbs, trunks, topple in a watery backwash.

When he goes to sleep, he says, the world stays in his head
like a big spiderweb strung between ear and ear,
buzzing like telephone wires, and what he has heard
all night, next morning has happened, is true, is there.

Though it always comes back for me, thick, bathed, grateful,
everything has to be re-imagined each sunrise
when I crawl from my black comfort. But I can't make a phone call.
I have to talk to something in front of my eyes.

You'd never know we were close. When we meet strangers
they poke my round stomach and pat his long bare legs,
I gush, and he, or that's what it looks like, glares,
then he stomps on my oils and we fight like cats and dogs.

87

But when it rains sometimes, and he feels it and I hear it,
and he closes my eyes with his fingers to stop my raining,
and one tear falls before everything is quiet,
and his tear is the color of cinnamon on my tongue,

oh then we leave together and nobody can find us.
Not even our mother, if she came, could tell us apart.
Only the stars can see, who cluster around us,
my painted person crouched in his painted heart.

Leda Reconsidered

She had a little time to think
as he stepped out of water
that paled from the loss of his whiteness
and came toward her.
A certain wit in the way he
handled his webbed feet,
the modesty of the light that lay on him,
a perfectly clear, and unforgivable,
irony in the cock of his head
told her more than he knew.
She sat there in the sunshine,
naked as a new-hatched bird,
watching him come,
trying to put herself
in the place of the cob, and see
what he saw:

flesh comfortable, used,
but still neatly following the bones,
a posture relaxed,
almost unseemly, expressing
(for the imagination,
unlike the poor body it strips and stirs,
is never assaulted)
openness, complicity even,
the look of a woman
with a context in which she can put
what comes next
(no chance of maiden's hysteria
if his beak pinched hold of her neck-skin,
yet the strangeness of the thing
could still startle her
into new gestures),
and something—a heaviness,

as if she could bear things,
or as if, when he fertilized her,
he were seeding the bank she sat on,
the earth in its aspect of
quiescence.

And now, how much would she try
to see, to take,
of what was not hers, of what
was not going to be offered?
There was that old story
of matching him change for change,
pursuing, and at the solstice
devouring him.
A man's story.
No, she was not that hungry
for experience. She had her loves.
To reimagine her life—
as if the effort were muscular
she lifted herself a little
and felt the pull at neck
and shoulderblade, back
to the usual.
And suppose she reached with practiced arms
past the bird, short of the god,
for a vulnerable mid-point,
and held on,
just how short-sighted would that
be? Would the heavens in a flurry record
a major injustice to the world's
possibilities?

He took his time,
pausing to shake out a wing.
The arrogance of that gesture!
And yet she saw him
as the true god.

She saw, with mortal eyes
that stung at the sight,
the pain of his transformations,
which, beautiful or comic,
came to the world
with the risk of the whole self.
She saw what he had to work through
as he took, over and over,
the risk of love,
the risk of being held,
and saw to the bare heart
of his soaring, his journeying,
his wish for the world
whose arms he could enter in the image
of what is brave or golden.

To love with the whole imagination—
she had never tried.
Was there a form for that?
Deep, in her inmost, grubby
female center
(how could he know that,
in his airiness?)
lay the joy of being used,
and its heavy peace, perhaps,
would keep her down.
To give: women and gods
are alike in enjoying that ceremony,
find its smoke filling and sweet.
But to give up was an offering
only she could savor,
simply by covering
her eyes.

He was close to some uncommitted
part of her.
Her thoughts dissolved and

fell out of her body like dew
onto the grass of the bank,
the small wild flowers,
as his shadow,
the first chill of his ghostliness,
fell on her skin.
She waited for him so quietly that
he came on her quietly,
almost with tenderness,
not treading her.
Her hand moved into the dense plumes
on his breast to touch
the utter stranger.

Bedtime Stories

1972

Bedtime Stories

So early into a big bed stowed out of sight,
child that I was, wide awake from the day, the day
of chiding and loneliness, unspent energy
in muscle and bone ("growing pains"), the day's light
still promising from the window, would toss and yell,
"Grandma, Grandma! Please come and sit by me.
Tell me a story! Tell me another story!"
All that was missed, radio, books, preschool,
hours of TV, music, long good-nights said,
the thrilling, calling, right-after-supper play
of the other kids in their far-off pom-pom-pullaway,
would come in the voice of an old woman by the bed.

Three

Such things there are, we don't know.
It makes a persond think all the time.
I can tell you one thing, though.

My mother's friend she lived in town, they told it,
it was in town yet,
that every night there come alwus such a big black cat
and walked "m'ow, m'ow" all around the house
when it come midnight.

And right next door was an old widow woman
wouldn't talk to nobody or nothin, but they never ketched
her doin nothin. They let her alone.

And every night the black cat would come "m'ow, m'ow."

And the friend my mother thought one day how she'd fix him
and she kept the washwater boilin
and at night when a black cat come, never come in the daytime,
sneaked her a kittle of water and leaned out the window
and throwed out washwater on it in the Lord's name.
And it *screamed,* screamed like I don't know what then,
yowled terrible loud, they could hear it in Heaven
almost. Oh I don't know,
I tell you it makes the shivers to come—
The next day the old widow woman
come out her house all humped up, and you know what?
She was scald on her face, her head,
right where the washwater flew.
And she never anymore come in the cat.

I tell you,
I never forgot that.

Oh they told it alwus us kids, we shouldn't tease,
the Devil might be there because
that old widow woman was really scald.
Oh *Kind,* there is more in this old world
than a persond knows.

Four

Oh well, they had such a big garden
about half a block purt' near, and on two side
was all currants, planted in currant bushes
and one row was yet planted in the middle—that is,
one row currants, and one row gooseberries.
One row gooseberries on the other side.
And then four rows of great big tame grapes
through the other side, the south side of the garden.
Do you think us kids could pick a bunch of grapes?
The folks thought they could sell 'em but they wouldn't get
to town in time and they'd all rot.
Sometimes Father would go out and cut us
a bunch or so, but us kids wouldn't dare to pick.
Them grapes all went to waste, peck after peck,
Father never bought no sugar.
Only thing they did do was make this sorghum molasses.
That I ate on our bread all year.

To school, when we was at school, we had white lard
and a little salt sprinkled over on our bread,
and that was what we eat at school.
Nowadays if folks can't have two, three thick on their bread
they go on relief and the govment spreads it all.

But believe me when the cherries was ripe,
then we had our time.
They was just by the bushel and bushel
and bushel. And the plums, by jinks, then we had our fill.
Apples we didn't have many, Father plant that,
a big orchard, but they wasn't bearin yet.

Five

That was in 1875, then we moved here
with five covered wagons and we had seven cows with us.
And then we'd have to walk by spells, we'd change off
and one would drive the cows and then the other
one would. We sure seen some tough
times, sometimes people would be nice
and sometimes they wouldn't. We had to sleep in three of
the covered wagons, and sometimes, I tell you,
it rained and dripped on our face.

We was on the road nine days.

One time we had a sick horse, and then
we stopped because it wouldn't walk anymore.
We stopped by a horse doctor, and when
he got the medicine ready and start to give it
the horse, it dropped down dead, the horse.
Then a big thunder shower came up and they had
to bury it in the rain, such rain
that the water came right through the house.
I laid on the floor and just got soaked.

You see, we went over the Mississippi River
with a steamboat from Savannah Illinois to Sebulah
Iowa. When we stopped at Savannah
we stopped at a stone quarry, great big high
one, maybe one hundred fifty feet high.
Then one of the men with us stepped to the hill
at the edge and looked, how deep it was, and the whole
thing gave way with him. A great big oak yet,
right at the back of him, and these limbs was hangin
down where he was. He just grabbed one
and saved from fallin one hundred fifty feet.

Sometimes, them old wolves would howl
so at night, and gee,
then I couldn't sleep at all.

One time we stopped at a town and was gonna buy
some feed for the horses, they wouldn't let us have it.
They wanted us to stay there all night
and land knows what they was goin to do with us.
And Uncle said we wouldn't stay, they wouldn't let
us buy the feed. We drove on couple miles further,
it was all wild timber and it got kind of late.
When we got through all the wild timber
we come to a nice great big farm place. We stopped there
and asked could we stay all night, and, oh, they sure
wanted us to stay there.
They opened the gate for us and started a fire
and we got our supper.
And then the whole family come out and one of the men
that was along with us could play the accordion
and sing so nice, and they listened to that.
We set up till midnight.

Six

That was in 1875, and we come through
another big timber and come to a farmhouse
that had lots of grapes. But they was a ways
from the house and two men that was with us
tried to snipe some and they got ketched.
The people act mean at first but they was good
after all, and let 'em have some like folks should.

The next day or so, I and my uncle had to drive
the cows, the covered wagons quite a ways ahead.
They come past one place there was a lot of tatoes
growin. Them two young men was so hungry and thought they'd
stop and dig some, we wouldn't have to buy
for supper. But then the man that owned the tatoes
ketched them. When Uncle and I
got there with the cows, that fellow was lookin at his tatoes
yet. He wanted to know if we were that outfit gone on
with the mover wagons, and we told him yes.
He told my uncle he'd ketched them two boys
was stealin his tatoes and he was gonna stop us
at the next town and settle with us but he never
showed up and we never seen him again.

I was just a kid, youngest of the three girls,
and we all had to sleep in the wagon box—the wagon
box, it was, it sure was no wider than
forty inch. And them other two big girls
got me in the middle and purt' near killed me off.
They slept all night and I couldn't rest, they was bother
me, so big and I just a kid. So I got
me a couple box in back of the wagon, off

from them, and that's where I slept on top.
I got me a blanket and I slept on top there.
I tell you, I had to sleep somewhere.

Then we didn't have no more trouble and we
had a lot of fun too, and we got to Ackley.

Seven

Well, that was Saturday, day before Easter.
You know Gust, he alwus said there
was no Easter Rabbit, that's what he said.
He alwus said it was us that did it, colored
them eggs. Well so then one day it was the day
before Easter, they hadda plant tatoes so Mother
took the two kids along in the fields, she helped
plant tatoes that day. I didn't have to.

And while they was gone I got busy.
Sewed them eggs in the purtiest pieces from prints,
just made six or seven.
I had them purty pieces from Mrs. Ribberger
and I sewed them on.
Ja, and I got some wood ashes and filled my pan
and I packed my eggs in there and cover
'em up with the wood ashes. And then pour
boilin water over it, boiled 'em good and hard
about six or seven minutes, they was good and hard.

Then I took 'em out and put 'em in cold water
and after that I took the cloth off and oh
wasn't they purty! Honest, the purtiest I ever
seen, oh they was purty. And then when I had 'em
all done and laid 'em away, well then after supper
they monkeyed around a little bit and they got so
tired, went to bed. And those kids was gonna be sure
and shake the ashes out of the stove so they'd be sure
I didn't boil any so that there was no fire.
Thought I'd make 'em yet when they got to sleep.

Well and then they went to bed.
After they had that shook out they went to bed.
And you know, ennahow, they had their

nests made in the wardrobe or what they call that,
and that big box below, kind of a drawer.
So when they was good upstairs why Father
made a big racket on the porch, and I had
all the eggs in their nests, laid 'em quick in their nests.
And Father made another big racket, that the Rabbit
went out again. Then Father called
'em down and they come head over heels downstair.
Ja, and then they looked in their nests and seen yet
them purty eggs. Then Gust and Anna alwus
went to Father, "Father, did the Easter Rabbit
lay them eggs?" "Yes." Then they'd run
alwus to Mother, "Mother, did the Easter Rabbit
lay them eggs? Did you see him?" "Yes."

Then Gust believed there was an Easter Rabbit,
cause nobody could color eggs like that.
That sure was fun.

Nine

That was my grandfather, nearly went to prison.
I'm your grandmother and he was my grandfather, so
you must say. In the Old Country, and they was poor
and then if they could get to a big town some way,
why you see they could buy things cheaper.
So he and another man, a friend of hisn
ennaway, I don't know who he was, they thought
they'd go to a bigger place and get stuff cheaper,
coffee and sugar and such thing like that.

And you see, they wouldn't dare to go to a big place,
they'd get watched, some officer or police
would watch for them alwus. Because these poor people
in the little towns, why they would all run
to big towns to trade, and that they wouldn't dare
to do, had to stay in their own town.

So him and the fella, they went to them big towns,
go in the daytime and sneak back at night.
And so when they come back with a load, they had bought
a lot of stuff, they got caught in this timber.
The officer ketched them there.
Well and they start to run and he after them
and this brushwood was all piled in piles,
and it was so pitch dark they hid in the brush piles.
And they hid under them.

Then that fella, police, he come along with his spear,
he couldn't find 'em any other place,
so he come to the piles where my grandfather
was in. And he stuck a spear in and the spear
just run whzzzz past his face.
Three, four times he stuck it in there
and the one time it just went past him.

The other fella didn't get it at all, that was with him.
Then you see they had to stick in there three,
four hours, the way he said, because the policeman
would stay there and watch first. And toward morning they
crawled out all right and safe. He saved his head.
They got their stuff all home too, he would say.
And then he would laugh, my grandfather.
"They didn't get me ennaways," he alwus said.
That's all there was in it, that's all I can remember.

Twelve

Ja, we had it hard.
No butter, Father'd hafta sell it, on our bread.
No oley then, like they got now,
and we never got no bread sugared.
If the horse was sick, sometimes us kids pulled the plow
just like we was horses. And Mother, when she had the kids
us kids took care of the baby, Mother in the field.
We took turns to rock the baby, and if somebody come,
horsedoctor or so, we got scared and hid
behind the cradle, company hardly ever come.
Ja, they don't do that way no more.
They got things so good, go to the dimestore, grocerystore.
We'd piece quilts, purty pieces people give us,
pick chickens for our featherbeds, stuff 'em with feather.
So cold it was, but we musn't make no fuss.
When thunderstorms come, rain would come in on our face.
Such good roofing they have now, folks clean.
Why, *Kind,* every week when I got big enough
I'd comb out the girls' hair over the hot stove
and the lice would fall out and spit on the stove.

Sometimes we thought we'd sure hafta die.
Sometimes so sick we sure didn't know what to do.
Well, we made it ennahow.

New Poems from
Merciful Disguises

1973

Peony Stalks

Peony stalks come up like red asparagus,
I said; my friend said they look like dogs' penises.
It was something misplaced I noticed, the color of a wound,
but she's right, it has something to do with love too in my mind.

In the peony bed in spring they bloody the ground.
Things go wrong. My neighbor goes mad. My dog is poisoned.
Last night I was told of a woman who dug seventy worms
daily to feed an unnested robin. One dreams

of these hard salvations. Yet now the robin returns
in the afternoon for his worms, and beats at the screens
in the evening to get to his perch in the cellar. They are wounded,
woman and bird are wounded. There is no end.

Who's found the proper place for love? I worry about you,
and about the uncared-for. There is a leak in my life now.
I watch a puppy chasing lightning bugs or butterflies,
plunging upward, and up, and up again, and besides he's

a sick puppy. Against intention, the feelings raise
a whole heavy self, panting and clumsy, into these
contortions. We live in waste. I don't know about you,
but I live in the feelings, they direct the contortions of the day,

and that is to live in waste. What we must do, we do,
don't we, and learn, in love and art, to see
that the peony stalks are red, and learn to say this
in the calm voice of our famous helplessness.

Midas and Wife

He loved the way her fingers loved the ground,
a peasant touch that patted things green,
and would tent to petition for the rain

that made their garden move, and reach freely
for bugs that burrowed or birds that flew away.
She loved his gift for making that fairness stay.

But, lest she stay, he couldn't touch the queen
in whose cold image creation could be undone.
He feared his fingers and their golden gain,

but followed her from room to room
to touch what she touched. She arranged a trembling bloom,
he touched; the flower fell into its form.

The dog quivered and smiled at her attention,
but felt his brilliant answer and soon
froze forever in a witty grin.

The years went by, and all she carried inside
to feel his sovereignty acquiesced and died
into perfection, and into the eternal married,

except herself. The heart of Midas grew cold
from his abstention, the queen grew old,
and the whole palace filled with scions of gold.

She spoke then: "Look at my face, Midas, my shame
shouts to you there of my long affair with time
while I yearned for the king whose art could keep me home.

I reach for you through the world, and you never come,
you reach for what I touch, not what I am,
and down between us falls your golden theme.

Besides, I have grown so fond of the rich and still,
though all outdoors rage with the green and fruitful
I cannot bear my own composure until

you hold me. Changing under your touch, I'll prove
whatever holds perfectly is stronger than love,
but subject still to love's artless imperative.

Never on earth, my dear, can you and I
discover a golden mediocrity.
The sovereign gift must find a way to comply."

When Midas moved in loneliness and pain
to touch her hand, her hand turned numb,
her heart turned quietly into a paradigm,

and she took her final form in idolatry.
Blinding, and blind to him, her sun-like eye,
but her brazen lips could move him anyway,

and Dionysus, smiling, set him free.

Economics

Out of a government grant to poets, I paid
to be flung through the sky from St. Louis to San Francisco,
and paid for tours and cruises and bars, and paid
for plays and picnics and film and gifts and the ho-

tel for two weeks, and all the niceties
of sea, field, and vineyard, and imports potted
and pickled and sugared and dried, and handouts for hippies,
and walking shoes and cable and cab, and, sated

with wild black blare, Brahms, marimba and Muzak,
and beaches, and cityscapes, uphill, downhill,
and colors of water, oil, neon, acrylic,
and coffees spiced, spiked, blazing, cool,

foamed, thick, clear, on the last night,
two extra suitcases packed to go home again,
with the last of the travellers' checks paid for eight
poets to dine with me in Chinatown:

hour after hour of rich imagery,
waiters and carts, delights of ceremony,
fire of sauce, shaped intricacy
of noodle and dumpling, the chicken cracked from clay,

its belly crammed with water chestnut and clam,
the shrimp and squid and lobster, the sweet and sour,
beer chill, broth and tea steam,
the great glazed fish coiled on its platter,

the chopped, the chunky, the salty, the meat, the wit,
the custard of almond and mint, the ginger cream,
the eloquent repletion I paid for . . . And yet,
did I spend enough in that city all that time

of my country's money, my country's right or wrong,
to keep one spoonful of its fire from eating
one hangnail, say, of one Vietcong?

"Don't clear the fish away yet," one poet said.
"The cheek of the fish is a great delicacy."
With a spoon handle he probed away in its head
and brought out a piece of white flesh the size of a pea.

"For the hostess," he said, "from all her grateful gourmets."
In SAVE THE CHILDREN ads I've seen the babies.
Filled with nothing but gas and sour juice,
their bellies bulge like rotten cabbages.

"One dollar to CARE will pay for ninety meals."
They cry. They starve. They're waiting. They are in anguish.
How can we bear to imagine how it feels?
Pain. *Pain.* I ate the cheek of the fish.

In an instant of succulence my hideous maw
swallowed, I'd guess, the dinners of fifty children.
What good does it do to really take that in,
and what good does it do to vomit it out again?

Gentle reader, should I economize?
I write poems for fifty cents a line.
This poem is worth what it's worth to the families
of two human beings under the age of eighteen

to see them blown to pieces. "Indemnification
for civilian casualties: from eight dollars
and forty cents for a wounded child, on
up to the top sum of thirty-three dollars

and sixty cents for a dead adult." I tipped
the waiter fifteen percent, which came to nine dollars.

The cab drive was a third of a child. I slept
each night for a fourth of his mother. What are dollars?

And what are words, as formed and plump on the page
as Chinese dumplings? Or love, that mink stole,
that sweepstakes prize for one in a million? What wage
could I ever earn that would let me afford to feel

how a newborn, somewhere, is learning to focus
on a world that drains its pus in his eyes like an eyesore?
Our right to see the beauties of this world grant us
that we may grant it, or
                              Christ, what are poems for?

The Talker

One person present steps on his pedal of speech
and, like a faulty drinking fountain, it spurts
all over the room in facts and puns and jokes,
on books, on people, on politics, on sports,

on everything. Two or three others, gathered
to chat, must bear his unending monologue
between their impatient heads like a giant buzz
of a giant fly, or magnanimous bullfrog

croaking for all the frogs in the world. Amid
the screech of traffic or in a hubbub crowd
he climbs the decibels toward some glorious view.
I think he only loves himself out loud.

The Cities of the Plain

Their sex life was their own business,
I thought, and took some of the pressure off women,
who were treated, most of the time, as merely
a man's way of producing another man.
And there were plenty of the other kind—
the two older girls got married when they wanted to.
The riot in front of our house that evening,
when a gang of young queers, all drunk and horny,
threatened to break in, yelling
for the two strangers, our guests, handsome
as angels, to come out and have some fun,
was not intelligently handled by my husband,
to say the least. An uptight man,
he got so frightened he opened the door
and offered to send out our youngest girls
if they'd quiet down and leave us alone.
"Two little virgins," he told them. "Now, fellows,
wouldn't that be nicer, and more fun?"
That made them wild, and they would have dragged
him out and mounted him in the street
if our guests hadn't managed to get the door shut.

The two strangers, it turned out, were Inspectors.
Don't ask me why, for the sake of a Perfect
Idea, of Love or of Human Community,
all the innocent-eyed, babies and beasts
and birds, all growth, both food and flower,
two whole cities, their fabulous bouquets
of persons, frivolous, severe, rollicking,
wry, witty, plain, lusty,
provident, every single miracle of life
on the whole plain should be exploded
to ashes. I looked back, and that's what I saw.

Nobody knows my name. My husband
and our two adolescents kept their faces
turned to the future, fled to the future.
Sarah everyone knows, whose life,
past menopause, into the withered nineties
was one long, obsessed attempt to get pregnant,
to establish the future. As for me, I lost
all sense of human possibility
when the cloud rose up like a blossom over all that
death. I stood for nameless women
whose sense of loss is not statistical,
stood for a while, then vanished. Men
are always being turned to stone by something,
and loom through the ages in some stony
sense of things they were shocked into.
I was not easily shocked, but that punishment
was blasphemous, impiety
to the world as it is, things as they are.
I turned to pure mourning, which ends the personal
life, then quietly comes to its own end.
Each time the clouds came and it rained,
salt tears flowed from my whole being,
and when that testimony was over
grass began to grow on the plain.

A Small Excursion

Take a trip with me
through the towns in Missouri.
Feel naming in all its joy
as we go through Braggadocio, Barks, Kidder, Fair Play,
Bourbon, Bean Lake,
and Loose Creek.
If we should get lost
we could spend the night at
Lutesville, Brinktown, Excello, Nodaway,
Humansville, or Kinderpost.

If we liked Bachelor we could bypass
with only slight compunction
another interesting place,
Conception Junction.

I think you would feel instant intimacy
with all the little flaws
of an Elmer, Esther, Ethel, Oscar, or Archie,
all the quirky ways
of a Eunice or a Bernice,
at home in a
Hattie or even an Amazonia.

I'd enjoy, wouldn't you, saying that I came from
Chloride, or Map or Boss or Turtle
or Arab or Chamois or Huzzah or Drum.

Surely the whole world loves the lover of men
who calls a tiny gathering
in midwest America
Paris, Carthage, or Alexandria,
Odessa, Cairo, Arcadia, or Milan,
as well as the one who calls

his clump of folk
Postoak,
the literalist who aims low
and calls it Shortbend or Old Mines
or Windyville or Iron or Nobby or Gumbo.

Riding along together,
we could think of all we'd had
at both Blooming Rose and Evening Shade.
Heading into the setting sun,
the gravel roads might get long and rough,
but we could make the difficult choice between
Minimum and Enough,
between Protem and Longrun.
And if it got very late
we could stay at Stet.

Isn't there something infinitely appealing
in the candor
of calling a collection of human beings
Liberal, Clever, Bland, or
Moody, Useful, Handy, or
Rich, Fertile, and Fairdealing?
People who named these towns
were nobody's fools.
Passing through Peculiar, we could follow
a real school bus labelled Peculiar Public Schools.

O to be physically and aesthetically
footloose,
travelling always,
going through
pure sound that stands for a space,
like Cabool, Canalou, Plad, Auxvasse,
Koshkonong, Weaubleau, Roubidoux,
Hahn Dongola, Knob Noster, and Foose!

End of May

Atop each stem
an iris or two has turned in
on itself with no regrets and given up
color. Pink, yellow, and red,
the rosepetals are spread
so wide they already tend
toward total drop.
Peony litter covers the ground.
On earlier days
friends and neighbors in pairs have been summoned
to have a drink and see the bloom,
have admired everything and gone.

I sit in my suntan oil alone—
almost alone—a jay
tries to flap me away
from his drinking trough.
His coarse, demanding rebukes
pierce my ears. He chirks
news of impending drought.

But under my feet as I tan
is no longer a brick patio,
rather a light brown
paisley made of seed wings
from the silver maple, which can sow
faster than I can sew
this fine fabric into something.
And in the air,
like a great snow,
are flakes alive with purpose.
The cottonwood huffs and puffs
them everywhere.

On oil that sheathes me from sun
they cling to bare parts of person.
All the long, late
day, my arms and legs are furred
with such a will to beget
I think I can almost afford
to forget it's only skin-deep.
It's like taking dope.

It's too late, I tell the tree,
you've settled on somebody seedless.
Equivocally, it nods its head.
But I have been overheard.
Maybe for you but not for me,
the seedy old world says.

What the Motorcycle Said

Br-r-r-am-m-m, rackety-am-m, OM, *Am:*
All—r-r-room, r-r-ram, ala-bas-ter—
Am, the world's my oyster.

I hate plastic, wear it black and slick,
hate hardhats, wear one on my head,
that's what the motorcycle said.

Passed phonies in Fords, knocked down billboards, landed
on the other side of the Gap, and Whee,
bypassed history.

When I was born (The Past), baby knew best.
They shook when I bawled, took Freud's path,
threw away their wrath.

R-r-rackety-am-m, *Am.* War, rhyme,
soap, meat, marriage, the Phantom Jet
are shit, and like that.

Hate pompousness, punishment, patience, am into Love,
hate middle-class moneymakers, live on Dad,
that's what the motorcycle said.

Br-r-r-am-m-m. It's Nowsville, man. Passed Oldies, Uglies,
Straighties, Honkies. I'll never be
mean, tired or unsexy.

Passed cigarette suckers, souses, motherfuckers,
losers, went back to Nature and found
how to get VD, stoned.

Passed a cow, too fast to hear her moo, "*I* rolled
our leaves of grass into one ball.
I am the grassy All."

Br-r-r-am-m-m, rackety-am-m, OM, *Am:*
All—gr-r-rin, oooohgah, gl-l-utton—
Am, the world's my smilebutton.

A View

You drive, the road aims for a mountain.
Down paving, toward the low basket of the sun,

a jackrabbit is dribbled by slaps of hot wind.
Hummocky, glazed, superficial, tanned

the landspread. I ride beside you, in the time
of life to note character, waiting for the sublime.

Enhancement of hills. Foisted up by their trite
avowals, we grow more close and hot.

Far ahead, something definite is about to occur.
The way goes flat, dusky. There they are,

the god, looming, and with him—but she is terrible!—
lying at his feet, his own foothill,

wrinkled, blue, balding, risen-above,
her back all sore from trails, child-ridden, shoved

to the ground in a dumpy heap, mined-out,
learned-on by the high one until that

moment he knew his own destiny, donned
a green-black cloak, rose up around

mid-life to stay with the stars, his face flint,
his eyes slatey and bland, and she went

into her change. Oh she was fanciful once,
garbed in dapples of yarrow, lupine and gentians,

silvery inside, always a-chatter
with rockchuck and nuthatch, point-breasted, and later

glad to be taken. Opened unmercifully,
she was used all over. Then, so accessible, she

was fair game for everyone. Even her shale
surfaces have been wrung out for oil.

He stands nearby, unmoved. He knows
how not to be. Even at sundown he flourishes.

He can sway in aspen and tender seedgrass
in his low meadows, wearing the disgrace

of his early delicacy still, where blue grouse,
calliope hummingbird, rosy finch rise

and fall in paintbrush, harebell, penstemon,
beeplant, columbine. Nothing is gone.

He shows without shame these young, soft
traces, having gone on to lift

into view rock ribs and evergreen
masculinity. He transcends every mine,

they are small scars in his potency, something
unearthly shocked, shook him and kept him ascending.

He grew rough, scrabbly, wore outlaw underbrush,
gray fox, bobcat and cougar, secret fish.

Then he was stale for a while, all bare bone, then reared
a feast of self in a head uncovered,

streaked gray and white, playing cool, leaning
on no shoulder, above raining,

oblivious of his past, in pride of escape.
Never downhearted, he is wholly grown up.

You turn and ask how I am. I say
I'm admiring the scenery, and am O.K.

Letters from a Father, and Other Poems

1 9 8 2

Letters from a Father

I

Ulcerated tooth keeps me awake, there is
such pain, would have to go to the hospital to have
it pulled or would bleed to death from the blood thinners,
but can't leave Mother, she falls and forgets her salve
and her tranquilizers, her ankles swell so and her bowels
are so bad, she almost had a stoppage and sometimes
what she passes is green as grass. There are big holes
in my thigh where my leg brace buckles the size of dimes.
My head pounds from the high pressure. It is awful
not to be able to get out, and I fell in the bathroom
and the girl could hardly get me up at all.
Sure thought my back was broken, it will be next time.
Prostate is bad and heart has given out,
feel bloated after supper. Have made my peace
because am just plain done for and have no doubt
that the Lord will come any day with my release.
You say you enjoy your feeder, I don't see why
you want to spend good money on grain for birds
and you say you have a hundred sparrows, I'd buy
poison and get rid of their diseases and turds.

II

We enjoyed your visit, it was nice of you to bring
the feeder but a terrible waste of your money
for that big bag of feed since we won't be living
more than a few weeks longer. We can see
them good from where we sit, big ones and little ones,
but you know when I farmed I used to like to hunt
and we had many a good meal from pigeons
and quail and pheasant but these birds won't

be good for nothing and are dirty to have so near
the house. Mother likes the redbirds though.
My bad knee is so sore and I can't hardly hear
and Mother says she is hoarse from yelling but I know
it's too late for a hearing aid. I belch up all the time
and have a sour mouth and of course with my heart
it's no use to go to a doctor. Mother is the same.
Has a scab she thinks is going to turn to a wart.

III

The birds are eating and fighting, Ha! Ha! All shapes
and colors and sizes coming out of our woods
but we don't know what they are. Your Mother hopes
you can send us a kind of book that tells about birds.
There is one the folks called snowbirds, they eat on the ground,
we had the girl sprinkle extra there, but say,
they eat something awful. I sent the girl to town
to buy some more feed, she had to go anyway.

IV

Almost called you on the telephone
but it costs so much to call thought better write.
Say, the funniest thing is happening, one
day we had so many birds and they fight
and get excited at their feed you know
and it's really something to watch and two or three
flew right at us and crashed into our window
and bang, poor little things knocked themselves silly.
They come to after while on the ground and flew away.
And they been doing that. We felt awful
and didn't know what to do but the other day
a lady from our Church drove out to call
and a little bird knocked itself out while she sat

and she brought it in her hands right into the house,
it looked like dead. It had a kind of hat
of feathers sticking up on its head, kind of rose
or pinky color, don't know what it was,
and I petted it and it come to life right there
in her hands and she took it out and it flew. She says
they think the window is the sky on a fair
day, she feeds birds too but hasn't got
so many. She says to hang strips of aluminum foil
in the window so we'll do that. She raved about
our birds. P.S. The book just come in the mail.

    v

Say, that book is sure good, I study
in it every day and enjoy our birds.
Some of them I can't identify
for sure, I guess they're females, the Latin words
I just skip over. Bet you'd never guess
the sparrows I've got here, House Sparrows you wrote,
but I have Fox Sparrows, Song Sparrows, Vesper Sparrows,
Pine Woods and Tree and Chipping and White Throat
and White Crowned Sparrows. I have six Cardinals,
three pairs, they come at early morning and night,
the males at the feeder and on the ground the females.
Juncos, maybe 25, they fight
for the ground, that's what they used to call snowbirds. I miss
the Bluebirds since the weather warmed. Their breast
is the color of a good ripe muskmelon. Tufted Titmouse
is sort of blue with a little tiny crest.
And I have Flicker and Red-Bellied and Red-
Headed Woodpeckers, you would die laughing
to see Red-Bellied, he hangs on with his head
flat on the board, his tail braced up under,
wing out. And Dickcissel and Ruby Crowned Kinglet
and Nuthatch stands on his head and Veery on top

the color of a bird dog and Hermit Thrush with spot
on breast, Blue Jay so funny, he will hop
right on the backs of the other birds to get the grain.
We bought some sunflower seeds just for him.
And Purple Finch I bet you never seen,
color of a watermelon, sits on the rim
of the feeder with his streaky wife, and the squirrels,
you know, they are cute too, they sit tall
and eat with their little hands, they eat bucketfuls.
I pulled my own tooth, it didn't bleed at all.

VI

It's sure a surprise how well Mother is doing,
she forgets her laxative but bowels move fine.
Now that windows are open she says our birds sing
all day. The girl took a Book of Knowledge on loan
from the library and I am reading up
on the habits of birds, did you know some males have three
wives, some migrate some don't. I am going to keep
feeding all spring, maybe summer, you can see
they expect it. Will need thistle seed for Goldfinch and Pine
Siskin next winter. Some folks are going to come see us
from Church, some bird watchers, pretty soon.
They have birds in town but nothing to equal this.

So the world woos its children back for an evening kiss.

Lives of the Poets

I was fortunate enough to have
a mother who on one occasion
encouraged me by commissioning
a poem. Newly married, I
was tackling my first teaching job
when a letter came which said, in part:
"As writing is so easy for you
I want you to write a poem about
the San Benito Ladies Auxiliary
that I belong to. Our club has twenty
members and we bake cute cookies
and serve them with coffee and do our sewing
at the meeting. We make stuffed animals
to give poor Texas kids at Xmas.
We meet on every other Wednesday.
Tell all that in the poem. Write
the poem to be sung to the tune
of Silent Night Holy Night
as that is the only song I have learned
to play so far on my accordion.
I want to play and sing it at
the club meeting. I could do it myself
of course but writing makes me nervous.
I'm sure you will do this for me because
it is so easy for you and I know
you wouldn't want me to get nervous.
I have to have it this week so I
can get it down pat for the next meeting."

In the midst of grading a hundred or so
freshman themes, trying to master
A Vision so I could teach Yeats, and reading

the output of my creative writing
class, I wrote the poem for her.
(Some of the rhymes were hard.) I'm only
sorry that I didn't keep
a copy, and that I missed the performance.

Growing Up Askew

They had the Boston Bull before I was born,
and Mother liked her far more than she liked me.
We both had a trick. When Mother shaved one forefinger
with the other and said, "Shame, *sha-a-me!*" Peewee
would growl and snap most amusingly right on cue.
I, when shamed in the same manner, would cry.
I see my error now, but what good does it do?

Photographs

"Take what you want, we'll throw the rest away.
The mice are building nests in the box, we don't
want that old stuff anymore." My father, 88,
kicks the box over to me with his good leg.
My mother sits on her pee-damp paper pad,
trying to take part. The box is jammed to the top
with photos and albums, dust and chewed-up rug wool.
I dump and sort. Their parents' wedding pictures
scorched on cardboard where dimly and patiently
they held their breaths and posed for the sulfurous flash—
the men perched rigid in wicker studio chairs,
the girls standing beside in long, dark,
serviceable, handsewn gowns, their faces
stiff and startled as a dahlia presented
in a frill of ruching or of tatted lace,
one hand on the husband's shoulder, where it stayed.
Then with their broods of children, young, half-grown,
grown, their faces turning stern, parental,
bodies swelling, then melting down. "Surely
you want this batch." My parents shake their heads.
They are nobody's children now, or mine perhaps.

Their brothers and sisters, the fat, self-righteous face
of Grace, the missionary, who told me, eight
years old, "You're a bad, *bad* girl to say 'my goodness.'
Do you know why?" "No." "Because Goodness is GOD!"
May, the educated one, capped, gowned,
adopted by a rich and childless aunt
and given "advantages." Brought back for dinner
once with her own siblings, she laughed and cried out,
pointing at Dad, "Look at that boy's big nose!"—
a story my father told with bitterness
till he was in his sixties. Cora, whose faith-healer

couldn't cure the cancer she hid from her doctor.
Brownie, whose beautiful dark eyes were closed
to near-blindness by their drooping lids when she fell
downstairs and struck her head as a young bride.
Al, lover of poop-pillows, plastic turds
and pop-up snakes, whose youthful high-jinks
twisted to drunkenness and kleptomania.
The others, too, outlived. "I'll take all these."
Their web of love and hate has been broomed away.

"Who's this young woman?" My mother holds the picture
up to her eyes and squints her best. Dad takes it.
"Oh, *I* know, Anna Meinberg, Mother's chum.
When I was courting I always had to bring
a man for Anna or Mother wouldn't go."
He laughs toward Mother, but she doesn't smile.
"Throw it away." They are not lovers now.

I sort in the dimming light. My mother dozes.
"Who are all these children, Dad?" "Must be
your mother's folks, some Richsmeier or Peters kids."
They sit patiently, brushed, told to hold still,
their legs in black stockings and feet in high-top shoes
stuck out in front of them, the button-eyed
babies in crocheted caps with ribbon pom-poms
on either ear, sacked in tucked gowns or naked
like rubber dolls, their faces plump possibility.
For all three of us, they go in a discard pile.

And now a precious stack, my parents themselves:
The boy with his plowing team, the young father
with pompadour, the deep family lines
already scored between brows. ("When I grow up
I'm going to marry Daddy!" Then Mother's jealous
"Well you can't. *I* married him." "Why can't
I marry him too?" "Because you *can't,* that's why!")

Posed proudly with his bantams, with his turkeys,
goats (he never lost his farmer's heart).
Small eyes that never saw another's pain
or point of view. ("Your mother's always complaining.
I've fed and clothed her all her life. What more
does she *want*?") Full lips that laid down the law for us.
Big feeder before his heart attack, his Santa
belly swells in the gas station uniform.
"You'll have to feed him good," his mother told
his bride. "If dinner's late just hurry and set
the table. He'll think the food is almost ready."
Pride in the stances. "My word's my bond. I've never
cheated man nor woman." Pride of place:
"All that education will make you Big-Headed."
"All that reading will make you lose your mind."
My mother, the youngest, the beauty of her clan,
minx who wooed big brother Al away
from Cora, his twin, and held him clutched lifelong
in mischief and complicity. Expressive
face I studied all my childhood to learn
if I was wrong or right, kept or cast out.
Best cook in town, best seamstress—not enough.
"I'd have been a great singer if I hadn't married."
"I could have been a nurse if I hadn't had you."
In a ruffled dustcap, her arms and lap piled full
of eleven puppies, then standing with a braid
of thick hair down to her knees, then bobbed, marcelled,
then permed—the lovely features never show
her "nerves," the long years of dissatisfaction,
the walks she took me on when I reached adolescence
and poured my hard ear full of my father's failings.
"Don't tell *me* about it, it's not my fault,
I didn't marry him!" "Mother, wake up.
I wish you could see this picture of your long hair."
"I could *sit* on my hair." The old boast comes by rote.
"You want to keep this batch a little longer, don't you?"
"No." Those faces have turned fictional.

And now their only child, long-legged, skinny
from trying to please and hardly ever pleasing.
Long curls my mother wound on rags for a while,
then highschool ugliness, then a fragile gauze
of beauty young womanhood laid on the lens, then lifted,
with my young husband slowly changing beside me,
my father's face stamped clearer and clearer on mine,
sterile publicity pictures, graying hair.
I need not ask the two frail watchers my question.
They are no longer parents. Their child is old.

The last's my ace—my father's great adventure
Suddenly he bought a housetrailer and pulled
his startled family from our Iowa village,
out of the cornfields and into the world's wonders,
all the way to Washington, then down
the California coast, then back to home,
packing a trunk so full of memories
they've lasted him for nearly fifty years.
The earth erupted for us all in moonscapes
of Black Hills, mountaintops hung from the sky
(the old Pontiac boiling on every pass),
Salt Lake held you up without an inner tube,
rodeos bucked in Wyoming, bears rocked the trailer
at night in national parks, great waterfalls roared,
Mother and I made snowballs in July
on Crater Lake and posed before studios
in Hollywood, we all stood on Boulder Dam,
our fan belt broke in the desert and Dad hitchhiked
while I fainted from the heat. On the desert, too,
in the one hundred twenty degree trailer, Mother
boiled potatoes and made gravy for dinner.
"If I don't get my spuds every noon I'll drive
us right back home!" We knew he meant what he said.
For years we all relived the trip, Dad using
the album to remind himself of stories,
used it to entertain any company—

old friends, then new ones elsewhere—then, years later,
the hired help of their old age. Still later
I'd use it to get him going, to cheer him up,
to distract him from worries, boredom, aches and pains.
I turn on the light. "Dad, here's our *trip*! Remember . . ."
He interrupts, staring at the darkened window,
"Everything's rusting away out in the garage.
It's been so long since I could get outside . . ."
My mother stirs. "When's the girl going to fix
my banana and coffee? I want to go back to bed."
I close the box. Somewhere a telephone
has made the appointment—a flower-scented pose
where they wait with patience for one witnessing heart
to snap its picture of their final faces.

The Stream

for my mother

Four days with you, my father three months dead.
You can't tell months from years, but you feel sad,

and you hate the nursing home. I've arranged a lunch
for the two of us, and somehow you manage to pinch

the pin from Madrid I bought you closed at the neck
of your best red blouse, put on new slacks, and take

off your crocheted slippers to put on shiny shoes,
all by yourself. "I don't see how you could close

that pin. You look so nice!" "Well, I tried and tried,
and worked till I got it. They didn't come," you said.

"Mother, I'm sorry, this is the wrong day,
our lunch is tomorrow. Here's a big kiss anyway

for dressing up for me. The nurse will come in
tomorrow and help you put on your clothes and pin."

"These last few days her mind has certainly cleared.
Of course the memory's gone," your doctor said.

Next day they bathed you, fixed your hair and dressed
you up again, got a wheelchair and wheeled you past

the fat happy babbler of nonsense who rolled her chair
all day in the hall, the silent stroller who wore

a farmer's cap and bib overalls with rows
of safety pins on the bib, rooms of old babies

in cribs, past the dining hall, on down to a sunny
lounge in the other wing. "Where can I pee,

if I have to pee? I don't like it here, I'm afraid.
Where's my room? I'm going to faint," you said.

But they came with the lunch and card table and chairs
and bustled and soothed you and you forgot the fears

and began to eat. The white tablecloth, the separate
plate for salad, the silvery little coffee pot,

the covers for dishes must have made you feel
you were in a restaurant again after all

those shut-in years. (Dad would never spend the money,
but long ago you loved to eat out with me.)

You cleaned your soup bowl and dishes, one by one,
and kept saying, "This is fun! This is *fun!*"

The cake fell from your trembly fork, so I fed
it to you. "Do you want mine, too?" "Yes," you said,

"and I'll drink your milk if you don't want it." (You'd
lost twelve pounds already by refusing your food.)

I wheeled you back. "Well, I never did *that* before!
Thank you, Jane." "We'll do it again." "Way down *there*,"

you marveled. You thanked me twice more. My eyes were wet.
"You're welcome, Mother. You'll have a good nap now, I'll bet."

I arranged for your old companion, who came twice a day,
to bring you milkshakes, and reached the end of my stay.

On the last night I helped you undress. Flat dugs
like antimacassars lay on your chest, your legs

and arms beetle-thin swung from the swollen belly
(the body no more misshapen, no stranger to see,

after all, at the end than at the beloved beginning).
You chose your flowered nightgown as most becoming.

You stood at the dresser, put your teeth away,
washed your face, smoothed on Oil of Olay,

then Avon night cream, then put Vicks in your nose,
then lay on the bed. I sat beside your knees

to say goodbye for a month. "You know I'll call
every Sunday and write a lot. Try to eat well—"

Tears stopped my voice. With a girl's grace you sat up
and, as if you'd done it lifelong, reached out to cup

my face in both your hands, and, as easily
as if you'd said it lifelong, you said, "Don't cry,

don't cry. You'll never know how much I love you."
I kissed you and left, crying. It felt true.

I forgot to tell them that you always sneaked your meat,
you'd bragged, to the man who ate beside you. One night

at home, my heart ringing with what you'd said,
then morning, when the phone rang to say you were dead.

I see your loving look wherever I go.
What is love? Truly I do not know.

Sometimes, perhaps, instead of a great sea,
it is a narrow stream running urgently

far below ground, held down by rocky layers,
the deeds of Mother and Father, helpless soothsayers

of how our life is to be, weighted by clay,
the dense pressure of thwarted needs, the replay

of old misreadings, by hundreds of feet of soil,
the gifts and wounds of the genes, the short or tall

shape of our possibilities, seeking
and seeking a way to the top, while above, running

and stumbling this way and that on the clueless ground,
another seeker clutches a dowsing-wand

which bends, then lifts, dips, then straightens, everywhere
saying to the dowser, it is there, it is not there,

and the untaught dowser believes, does not believe,
and finally simply stands on the ground above,

till a sliver of stream finds a crack and makes its way,
slowly, too slowly, through rock and earth and clay.

Here at my feet I see, after sixty years,
the welling water—to which I add these tears.

In the Missouri Ozarks

Under an overwashed, stiff, gray
sheet of sky, the hills
lie like a litter of woodchucks,
their backs mottled black with leafless
branches and brown with oakleaves,
hanging on till spring.
Little towns are scabs in their haunches.

Out of the hills the pickups scuttle
like water beetles onto the highway,
which offers up STUCKEY'S, EATS,
GOD'S WELL, CAVES,
JUNQUE, HOT BISCUITS 'N'
CREAM GRAVY, $6. OVERNIGHT
CABINS and a WINERY
to the chilled traveller.

Town leads off with a garish motel,
followed by the Shopping Plaza—
a monster of a supermarket
and a few frail shops; then comes
the courthouse square, with a barnfaced
Dollar Department Store,
Happy's Hardware and TV,
Shorty's Beer-Cafe,
two quiet banks and a chiropractor.
Big white gingerbreaded houses
and new ranchstyles
fizzle out on the edge of town
to yellow, brickpatterned tarpaper
shacks, leaning against the firewood
stacked as high as their roofs.

Off the highway, frosty weeds
lift berries and pods

on either side of the road in a mileslong
wine and black and beige bouquet,
and every twenty acres or so
a fieldstone cottage
guards its pastured cows
and its woods of oak and black walnut.
Farm dogs explode from porches
and harry the car down the gravel,
yipping at stones spat from the wheels.
Out here, after the supper dishes,
three or four couples will walk down the road
to a neighbor's, and will sit
around the heating stove,
talking about Emma Harbis,
who is finally giving away cuttings
of her famous orange-blooming
Kalanchoë, and about the Ed Lelands,
on food stamps all year,
but with a brand-new pickup
parked bold as brass
in their front yard, and about
Old Lady Kerner, who was seen
in the drugstore buying Oil of Olay
to smooth out the wrinkles
eighty-two hard years have hammered
into her indomitable face.

Moose in the Morning, Northern Maine

At six a.m. the log cabins
nose an immense cow-pie of mist
that lies on the lake.
Nineteen pale goldfinches perch
side by side on the telephone wire
that runs to shore,
and under them the camp cow,
her bones pointing this way and that,
is collapsed like a badly constructed
pup tent in the dark weeds.
Inside, I am building a fire
in the old woodstove with its rod overhead
for hunters' clothes to steam on.
I am hunting for nothing—
perhaps the three cold pencils
that lie on the table like kindling
could go in to start the logs.
I remember Ted Weiss saying,
"At the exhibition I suddenly realized
Picasso had to remake everything he laid his eyes on
into an art object.
He couldn't let the world alone.
Since then I don't write every morning."

The world is warming and lightening
and mist on the pond
dissolves into bundles and ribbons.
At the end of my dock there comes clear,
bared by the gentle burning,
a monstrous hulk with thorny head,
up to his chest in the water,
mist wreathing round him.
Grander and grander grows the sun
until he gleams, his brown coat

glistens, the great rack,
five feet wide, throws sparks
of light. A ton of monarch,
munching, he stands spotlit.
Then slowly, gravely, the great neck lowers
head and forty pounds of horn
to sip the lake.
The sun stains the belittled
cow's hide amber.
She heaves her bones and bag
and her neckbell gongs
as she gets to her feet
in yellow blooms of squaw-weed.
On the telephone wire
all the little golden bells are ringing
as that compulsive old scribbler, the universe,
jots down another day.

The Learners

We slapped the smirking mother
and the swollen father
and went to live in museums
and anthologies. Around us
were images of such fairness
that the world outside
was smoothed into smog.
We knew it was hard.
We were bony and strong
but our knuckles broke
as we cleaned and copied.

When rocks split the cellophane windows
we stumbled outside
leading the eldest.
Sun seared our eyeballs
and the cramp of the journey
crazed some of the seemliest.
Some of us dried to jerky.
When the light lowered a bit
some of us said they found
beauty beyond belief
in the ashes and oilspills.

When darkness came down
some mated, some murdered each other.
Some of us shook our fists
at the moon and the stars
for disdainful distance.
All over creation
there were sounds and shadows.
Digging into a cockpit of earth
with our broken knuckles
some of us sat and waited
with whatever was in the world.

Caring for Surfaces

Birds build but not I build, no, but wipe, Time's wife.
Dipped in detergent, dish and chandelier retrieve
their glister, sopped, kitchen floor reflowers, knife
rubbed with cork unrusts, colors of carpetweave
cuffed with shampooer and vacuum will reblush,
prints sprayed and scrubbed no longer peer but stare,
buffed, silver burns, brushed, plaster will gush
hue at you, tops soothed with cloth will clear.

Cleansing the cloud from windows, I let the world win.
It comes in, and its light and heat heave the house,
discolor, dim, darken my surfaces. Then once again,
as for forty years, my fingers must make them rouse.

Round rooms of surfaces I move, round board, books, bed.
Men carve, dig, break, plunge as I smooth, shine, spread.

The Vision Test

My driver's license is lapsing and so I appear
in a roomful of waiting others and get in line.
I must master a lighted box of far or near,
a highway language of shape, squiggle and sign.
As the quarter-hours pass I watch the lady in charge
of the test, and think how patient, how slow, how nice
she is, a kindly priestess indeed, her large,
round face, her vanilla-pudding, baked-apple-and-spice
face in continual smiles as she calls each "Dear"
and "Honey" and shows first-timers what to see.
She enjoys her job, how pleasant to be in her care
rather than brute little bureaucrat or saleslady.
I imagine her life as a tender placing of hands
on her children's hands as they come to grips with the rocks
and scissors of the world. The girl before me stands
in a glow of good feeling. I take my place at the box.
"And how are *you* this lovely morning, Dear?
A few little questions first. Your name?—Your age?—
Your profession?" "Poet." "What?" She didn't hear.
"Poet," I say loudly. The blank pink page
of her face is lifted to me. *"What?"* she says.
"POET," I yell, "P-O-E-T."
A moment's silence. *"Poet?"* she asks. "Yes."
Her pencil's still. She turns away from me
to the waiting crowd, tips back her head like a hen
drinking clotted milk, and her "Ha ha hee hee hee"
of hysterical laughter rings through the room. Again
"Oh, ha ha ha ha hee hee hee."
People stop chatting. A few titter. It's clear
I've told some marvelous joke they didn't quite catch.
She resettles her glasses, pulls herself together,
pats her waves. The others listen and watch.
"And what are we going to call the color of your hair?"
she asks me warily. Perhaps it's turned white

on the instant, or green is the color poets declare,
or perhaps I've merely made her distrust her sight.
"Up to now it's always been brown." Her pencil trembles,
then with an almost comically obvious show
of reluctance she lets me look in her box of symbols
for normal people who know where they want to go.

The Ballad of Blossom

The lake is known as West Branch Pond.
It is round as a soapstone griddle.
Ten log cabins nose its sand,
with a dining lodge in the middle.

Across the water Whitecap Mountain
darkens the summer sky,
and loons yodel and moose wade in,
and trout take the feathered fly.

At camp two friendly characters
live out their peaceful days
in the flowery clearing edged by firs
and a-buzz with bumblebees:

Alcott the dog, a charming fool
who sniffs out frog and snake
and in clumsy capering will fall
from docks into the lake,

and Blossom the cow, whose yield is vaunted
and who wears the womanly shape
of a yellow carton badly dented
in some shipping mishap,

with bulging sack appended below
where a full five gallons stream
to fill puffshells and make berries glow
in lakes of golden cream.

Her face is calm and purged of thought
when mornings she mows down fern
and buttercup and forget-me-not
and panties on the line.

Afternoons she lies in the shade
and chews over circumstance.
On Alcott nestled against her side
she bends a benevolent glance.

Vacationers climb Whitecap's side,
pick berries, bird-watch, or swim.
Books are read and Brookies fried,
and the days pass like a dream.

But one evening campers collect on the shelf
of beach for a comic sight.
Blossom's been carried out of herself
by beams of pale moonlight.

Around the cabins she chases Alcott,
leaping a fallen log,
then through the shallows at awesome gait
she drives the astonished dog.

Her big bag bumps against her legs,
bounces and swings and sways.
Her tail flings into whirligigs
that would keep off flies for days.

Then Alcott collects himself and turns
and chases Blossom back,
then walks away as one who has learned
to take a more dignified tack.

Next all by herself she kicks up a melee.
Her udder shakes like a churn.
To watching campers it seems she really
intends to jump over the moon.

Then she chases the cook, who throws a broom
that flies between her horns,

and butts at the kitchen door for a home,
having forgotten barns.

Next morning the cow begins to moo.
The volume is astounding.
MOOOAWWW crosses the lake, and MAWWWW
from Whitecap comes rebounding.

Two cow moose in the lake lift heads,
their hides in sun like watered
silk, then scoot back into the woods,
their female nerves shattered.

MOOOAWWW! and in frightened blue and yellows
swallows and finches fly,
shaping in flocks like open umbrellas
wildly waved in the sky.

In boats the fishermen lash their poles
and catch themselves with their flies,
their timing spoiled by Blossom's bawls,
and trout refuse to rise.

MAWWOOOO! No one can think or read.
Such agony shakes the heart.
All morning Alcott hides in the woodshed.
At lunch, tempers are short.

A distant moo. Then silence. Some said
that boards were fitted in back
to hold her in, and Blossom was led
up a platform into the truck,

where she would bump and dip and soar
over many a rocky mile
to Greenville, which has a grocery store
as well as the nearest bull.

But the camp is worried. How many days
will the bellowing go on?
"I hope they leave her there," one says,
"until the heat is gone."

Birds criss-cross the sky with nowhere to go.
Suspense distorts the scene.
Alcott patrols on puzzled tiptoe.
It is late in the afternoon

when back she comes in the bumping truck
and steps down daintily,
a silent cow who refuses to look
anyone in the eye.

Nerves settle. A swarm of bumblebees
bends Blue-eyed grass for slaking.
A clink of pans from the kitchen says
the amorous undertaking

is happily concluded. Porches
hold pairs with books or drinks.
Resident squirrels resume their searches.
Alcott sits and thinks.

Beads of birds restring themselves
along the telephone wire.
A young bull moose in velvet delves
in water near the shore.

Blossom lies like a crumpled sack
in blooms of chamomile.
Her gaze is inward. Her jaw is slack.
She might be said to smile.

At supper, laughter begins and ends,
for the mood is soft and shy.

One couple is seen to be holding hands
over wild raspberry pie.

Orange and gold flame Whitecap's peak
as the sun begins to set,
and anglers bend to the darkening lake
and bring up a flopping net.

When lamps go out and the moon lays light
on the lake like a great beachtowel,
Eros wings down to a fir to sit
and hoot* like a Long-eared owl.

* *The Long-eared owl's hoot resembles the whistle of tribute to the sight of something beautiful and sexy:* wheé *whée-you.*

Near Changes

1990

Birthstones

When I was young and we were poor
my mother showed me a ring some old love gave her,
and said, "I'll have your birthstone set in it."

And said, "Don't ever lose it. The jeweler
offered to sell me half-glass, half-emerald,
but I'm giving you the real jewel."

I wore it as if she had given me the world.
I had no notion what things cost.
I thought she'd love me if I could be good at last,

but I never was. When I thought I knew her face
I told her I realized that stone was glass.
She blushed, and said the jeweler must have lied.

I looked in books to find out how to feel.
Then, holding them cheap, I tried an exchange of rings.
My new one tested real.

And on I went, and learned to recognize
the faintest glimmer of pure green
in a hand's clasp, or a pair of eyes,

and out came carats of green from a guarded mine
in grateful exchange, and back came green in turn.
When I looked again I was grown,

and my fingers were decked with rings, and still more green
exchanges came, and we dropped them on the ground
as our hands filled and boxes filled,

and they roll and shine as far as I can see.
Dazzled I walk the world my mother gave me,
whose stony streets are paved with emerald.

[1966]

Late Loving

What Christ was saying, what he meant [in the story of Mary and Martha] was that the pleasures of that hair, that ointment, must be taken. Because the accidents of death would deprive us soon enough. We must not deprive ourselves, our loved ones, of the luxury of our extravagant affections. We must not try to second-guess death by refusing to love the ones we loved. . . .

MARY GORDON, Final Payments

If in my mind I marry you every year
it is to calm an extravagance of love
with dousing custom, for it flames up fierce
and wild whenever I forget that we live
in double rooms whose temperature's controlled
by matrimony's turned-down thermostat.
I need the mnemonics, now that we are old,
of oath and law in rememorizing that.
Our dogs are dead, our child never came true,
I might use up, in my weak-mindedness,
the whole human supply of warmth on you
before I could think of others and digress.
"Love" is finding the familiar dear.
"In love" is to be taken by surprise.
Over, in the shifty face you wear,
and over, in the assessments of your eyes,
you change, and with new sweet or barbed word
find out new entrances to my inmost nerve.
When you stand at the stove it's I who am most stirred.
When you finish work I rest without reserve.
Daytimes, sometimes, our three-legged race seems slow.
Squabbling onward, we chafe from being so near.
But all night long we lie like crescents of Velcro,
turning together till we readhere.
Since you, with longer stride and better vision,
more clearly see the finish line, I stoke

my hurrying self, to keep it in condition,
with light and life-renouncing meals of smoke.
As when a collector scoops two Monarchs in
at once, whose fresh flights to and from each other
are netted down, so in vows I re-imagine
I re-invoke what keeps us stale together.
What you try to give is more than I want to receive,
yet each month when you pick up scissors for our appointment
and my cut hair falls and covers your feet I believe
that the house is filled again with the odor of ointment.

Views

I fly all the time, and still I'm afraid to fly.
I need to keep both feet on the ground, the earth
within reach of my eyes. In airports I comfort myself
by assessing others—look at that handsome necktie,
the weave of that suit, the portfolio (people of worth
are going to be on this plane), the pearls on that shelf
of expensive bosom, the hairdresser's art! All this
tells my shuddering spirit that God wouldn't tip
my seatmates, all these important people, from sight.
Once the stewardess passed the word that Liz
would be joined in Rome by Richard Burton, who was up
in First Class. I have never felt so safe on a flight.

SECOND POET:

I too fly all the time, and still I tremble.
I arrive too early and sit there sweating and cold.
I read at a book but can't make out what it means.
I look around at the others as they assemble
and make a collection of the dowdy old,
backpacking young, slouched in their dusty jeans,
men who have business suits of the wrong size on,
Frizzled Hair, Greasy Hair, and Drooping Hem.
Humbly they live and humbly they will die—
this scroungiest bunch of people I've ever laid eyes on.
Surely God has no special fate in mind for *them,*
I tell myself, like a plane falling out of the sky.

Pigeon Eggs

for Peggy

"Some days, these days, the world's too hot to handle,
or cold, I guess I mean, too cold to kindle.

The next-door neighbor called: 'Peggy, your cats
your three damned cats have killed a rabbit!' That's

in the morning, it was lying in her backyard.
I got the spade—when it's dead it isn't hard—

but it moved, it was still alive! I took it home
on the spade, and waited with it till Howard came,

because Jeremy's had our Merc since he totalled his.
The rabbit was squeaking but Howard couldn't face

it either, so I borrowed the neighbor's Corvette
and drove the rabbit on the spade to the vet

for a shot. Coming home, at the busiest time of day,
a poodleish dog was running every-which-way

in the traffic, so I pulled to the side and got out
and dodged the cars and chased it down all right

and carried it into the car. Thank God for a tag!
I found the place, nobody home, closed the dog

in the back fenced yard and went home to have a drink.
Howard was playing Bach. Surely, you'd think,

my day was over, but you're wrong. My Bert,
my big yellow cat, had something that was hurt

outside the kitchen window. I chased him away
and it was a pigeon. You know what they always say,

things come in threes. I keep a box for birds
in the basement. I tell you I simply don't have words

for what happened next. I looked in the evening and there
was the pigeon, still alive, and I washed my hair

and did the dishes and straightened and went to bed,
and in the morning there was the pigeon, dead,

but before she died she had laid an egg. And it
was there in the box, stone cold. I thought, *Bullshit!*

How could I help but think of another time?
It was the same, but it was not the same.

We live, but our lives go on beyond our hands.
We tell, but we tell to no one who understands.

In our youth I put a pigeon in the box.
The world was hot, with the charming heat of sex,

and before the pigeon died she laid an egg.
The egg was warm when I found it. Mona, I beg

to defend that windowed world. I put it between
my breasts—the warm pigeon egg—all I had seen

and felt led me to believe in the coming birth.
I believed—and believe—I tell you for what it's worth.

I hardly knew the world and its funny ways.
Then Howie came home and hugged me! Those were the days!"

In Bed with a Book

In police procedurals they are dying all over town,
the life ripped out of them, by gun, bumper, knife,
hammer, dope, etcetera, and no clues at all.
All through the book the calls come in: body found
in bed, car, street, lake, park, garage, library,
and someone goes out to look and write it down.
Death begins life's whole routine to-do
in these stories of our fellow citizens.

Nobody saw it happen, or everyone saw,
but can't remember the car. What difference does it make
when the child will never fall in love, the girl will never
have a child, the man will never see a grandchild, the old maid
will never have another cup of hot cocoa at bedtime?
Like life, the dead are dead, their consciousness,
as dear to them as mine to me, snuffed out.
What has mind to do with this, when the earth is bereaved?

I lie, with my dear ones, holding a fictive umbrella,
while around us falls the real and acid rain.
The handle grows heavier and heavier in my hand.
Unlike life, tomorrow night under the bedlamp
by a quick link of thought someone will find out why,
and the policemen and their wives and I will feel better.
But all that's toward the end of the book. Meantime, tonight,
without a clue I enter sleep's little rehearsal.

Near Changes

from "The Year's Top Trivia,"
SANFORD TELLER, *Information Please Almanac,* 1979

"Bob Holt, a 20-year-old Seattle man,
was quietly walking on a downtown street,
disguised as a mallard duck,
when he was—for no apparent reason—
attacked by a husky, 6-foot-tall
bearded stranger.
The perpetrator spun him around by one wing,
tore off his duck bill,
hit him over the head with it,
and ran away.
Holt, who was dressed as a duck
to promote a local radio station,
had no explanation for the incident.
He told police,
'I didn't speak to him.
I didn't flap my wings
or do anything like that.' "

Is this trivia, after all,
or a profound story?
The gods used to do it,
to themselves and to mortals,
sometimes in mercy,
sometimes out of blind and merciless power,
but the rest of us only yearn in odd moments
of our fixed lives for the sense of it,
of how it would feel to be bull or swan
or obsessively weaving spider or even
the plucked and plundered
tree of bay,

for "Emerging from one's own self . . . ," says Llosa,
"is a way . . . of experiencing
the risks of freedom."
With the help of paper feathers
supplied by a local radio station,
settling into his new shape,
having become green-headed, rufous-breasted,
with bold white neckring and yellow bill,
walking quietly along,
a Seattle man began to turn avian
on a downtown street,
though the metamorphosis was only half-completed
since he could not quite say later,
"I didn't quack at him,"
but could say to fact-finders, "I didn't flap my wings
or do anything like that."

And the bearded stranger?
Prescient as Leda, he sensed the presence
which to others was not apparent,
and was only protecting his nest,
the brick and concrete of Sears and service stations
where the arm that ends in four fingers
and an opposable thumb
at one touch of a button
warms and cools the vulnerable flesh
and the brain in its dear, lip-voiding box of language
and lights the concealments of space
and brings forth the cadence of cars
and Beethoven to cover
the soundless spin of the globe
whose button is beyond its reach,
lest that nest return, at the wingéd touch
of the human imagination,
which transforms past belief,
sometimes in mercy,

sometimes in blind mercilessness,
to vast and silent waters
toward whose reedy edge
Bob Holt was coasting in for a landing,
without flapping his wings.

To a Friend Who Threw Away Hair Dyes

Surely history's seen a happy ruler!
Tell me the long wait that breaks the pride
and will, yet may end in mastery, is not vain,
that Time may love and take for royal bride
his humblest servant, and in exchange I'll tell you
that the heart's multitudes lower their eyes and bow down
at their first sight on the balcony of a beautiful,
brilliant head wearing its first cold crown.

Gardens (ADDENDUM FOR A FUTURE VISIT TO THE HECHT STUDY)

for Anthony Hecht

I

Someone once described the Japanese garden
as "trivialities arranged to look
significant." So might we label one kind
of poem, whose dry hint of a river or brook,
raked free of detritus, briefly flows, turns
into terraces (abstraction of waterfall)
and comes to its end in a large, strict rectangle
of the same white sand (the sea, the All
or Nothingness), whose stone showing its white
above the moss that wraps its lower part
can be read as a high mountain, forested
and snowcapped, in this metaphoric art.
Guided by its setting in white space
proportionally vast, the making mind
of the beholder, which walks hand in hand
with the austere creator, fast will find
one dwarf pine's looming. Shading, importance, meaning
tower from the green suggestion. Delicacy
molds throughout a narrow path between Nature's
carelessness and the lifeless rigidity
of perfect order. A world is here that returns
to pure idea when we look away,
its grasp on our hearts being as miniature
as the memory of one faultless, serene day.

II

But there is another kind of garden, another
poetry (might we say?) whose "mimicry

of endlessness" calls upon every muscle
of self, while the senses are whelmed toward idolatry.
To enter its rich acreage is to know
that much must be left for another day, or year
or season. Though Flora stands in stone, her kingdoms
of brilliant imagery cloud over or clear—
rosebeds, meadows of daffodil, rainbow
borders, wild blooms under treeshade—as time, as the sun,
changes their tourist. Next, breath-taking steeps and valleys;
then a Grotto for those the passage has undone,
attended by a kind-faced river-god.
Then, for sheer swagger, creation clipped to dream,
the topiary-work, the artist's little
joke on Nature, horse-play with be and seem.
Courage challenged, trusting the maker, one
may enter a Maze and step by step, deeper
into bewilderment, find in the yews
the cool and colder rehearsal of the sleeper
who loses in darkness time, place, others,
sense of self. But no, this is not that last
labyrinth of Minotaur or tomb,
and a string one hadn't noticed leads back fast,
the strong string that ties art to serious play.
And now the woods, where "art is used but to
conceal art." Light and dark and the dapple
of both are inside. Here and there a few
bright lines of birches sketch the merest hint
of happiness for all lost children, old
and young, scattering breadcrumbs in hope of home,
for lovers meeting in secret, Tristan, Isolde.
Strange, rare trees have been planted to look
at home with the colloquial. Deep
but penetrable, the woods release their guest,
having shown him beds of fern and heart's-ease they keep.
What loving lavishness creates such gardens—
worlds of thought and feeling as real as the world?
It is late. One stops and rests near a flowery fountain,

thinking with joy of what the tour unfurled,
thoughts that turn one's head toward a last far view,
the eye being led uphill by an aisle of green
between marbles of calm Athena and hurrying Eros
where the beautiful Folly of having lived can be seen.

The Insight Lady of St. Louis on Zoos

(a found oral poem)

The other day I had an insight.
I suddenly realized why I hate zoos.
You know how they build those enclosures
for an animal or two, and if the animal
is the kind that lives in a rocky country
they put one rock with it and then they say,
see, there it is in its natural habitat?
And if the animal is a forest animal
they plant one tree with it and then they say,
see, there it is in its natural habitat?
Well, the handyman had put up the new bookshelf
on the only wall in the house
that isn't already covered with bookshelves,
and I organized all the books I had used
to write my book on Svevo, and then
all the books I had used for my book on Kierkegaard,
and then I saw myself as a zoo animal.
They would build a bare room with three bare walls
and put me and one book in it and then they would say,
see, there she is in her natural habitat!

And that evening I went to a party
and when we left I went upstairs to get my own coat,
and you should have seen that upstairs—
how can people live in a mess like that?—
it looked as if the drugbusters had made a raid
and left every drawer half open
with the clothes and stuff dumped out on the floor,
and there was one book lying on the floor
and I picked it up to see what it was,
and then I had another terrible insight.
I knew what book they would put in my zoo pen.
It would be that book, *Building Bicycles*.

The Block

Childless, we bought the big brick house on the block,
just in case. We walked the dog. Mornings the women
looked up from their clipping and pruning and weeding
to greet us, at dusk the men stopped their mowing to chat.
The children were newly married or off to college,
and dogs they had left behind them barked from backyards
at our dog, first in warning, later in greeting.
On other blocks we walked in the zany blare
of adolescent records and stepped around skates
and tricycles left on the sidewalk, but our middle-aged block,
busy and quiet, settled us into its solace.

The years bloomed by. The old dogs were put to sleep.
We bought a scoop to walk our new pup on his leash
as the block turned newly cranky about its curbs.
A lucky few dragged a staggering grandchild on visit
up and down, shyly accepting praise.
The wife on the corner shovelled their snow. "They say
it's what kills the men. I won't take a chance with my husband."
Then bad news began to come, hushed voices passed it
across back fences, the job of collecting for plants
found its permanent volunteer on the block. Later
more flowers, and one left alone in some of the houses.
Salads and cakes and roasts criss-crossed the street.

Then the long, warm, secret descent began
and we slid along with it. "We need a last dog," I said,
"but I can't face it." My husband became the husband
of the widows on either side in his husbandly tasks
of lifting and drilling for pictures and fixing faucets,
and a kindly old handyman took over, house by house,
the outdoor chores of mowing and small repairs.
"What would we do without Andrew?" everyone said.
The graying children came oftener, checking on things.

One widower wanted to marry the widow next door,
but "I'm through with *that* business!" she told him. The lone lesbian
kept up her house, but nearly wrinkled away.
I turned my flower borders to beds of groundcover.

The end came before we knew it. All in one year
my husband retired and half of the houses emptied.
Cancer ate four, heart attacks toppled some others,
a nursinghome closed over one, the rest caned off
to apartments with elevators. For Sale signs loomed
like paper tombstones on the weedy lawns.
The gentle years turned vicious all of a sudden.
"I can't believe it," we said. "The block's gone.
No one buys houses now." Those of us left
drew close, exchanged keys "in case something happens."
The wealthy patriarch sat all day on his porch
across the street and watched the distant disaster.
"He's way in his nineties," our busybody reported.
"His day and night nurses keep leaving, he's so awful.
And he won't take his pills. He just says, 'What does it matter?' "

We left on a long vacation. Home to the block,
we saw For Sale signs gone, heard new dog voices.
Bedding plants sucked up color from the old soil.
"The block is filled with young families. Everything's changed,"
we heard right away. A flyer stuck in the door:
"Block Party Sunday. Street Blocked Off All Day.
Bring Something to Share. All Bikes and Trikes Are Welcome."
"Oh Lord, do we have to go to all that bedlam?"
my husband said. "Oh God, I think they eat
hot dogs or something like that," I said. Too late,
Time, in its merciless blindness, gave us children.

Memoir

for Harry Ford

As the conch tells the human ear,
silence wants to be sound,
so the earshell beseeches the eye
to find the sounds it would lose,
and the eye prays that flying words
will be trapped in the amber of print.

Like a pine the man who will print
what plays through his needle-branched ear
towers, his resin wraps words
and the resonant shape of their sound
that a dry heart has to let loose.
He will pass through art's strict needle's eye.

When the poem arrives at the eye
of the hurricane, hush of print
retrieves what the blind wind would lose.
Then the heart becomes all ear
and the deaf-mute world hears the sound
of its own green, resplendent words.

Who gives up the world for words
gives creation a bad black eye
in uncoupling sense and sound.
Detective Time takes his voiceprint,
which ends behind bars. Nature's ear
knows it was little to lose.

The heart must be mud-mum or lose
face when the god without words,
with child-cheeks, with Orphic ear,
lies down there, shuttered of eye,

and leaves his indelible imprint.
Love's incoherence is sound.

In a deathly silence, what sound
amends Time's law that we lose?
That memoir read from fine print,
love's beautiful babble its Foreword,
while art fixes the world I-to-eye.
Then breath beats the drum of our ear.

Sound ear and sound eye keep in print
any rhyme the world makes with its words
that the heart cannot bear to lose.

Headlines

The great black bellow tells us together
to be moved, to move. Interlocked into
a mega–jigsaw puzzle, rigid
as tenet, we begin a glacial slide
that crushes contours, countries, carries us
to importance, from daily to the eternal.
The Big Picture, we model behind us
mountains of death, foothills of hunger,
meadows of merriment, chasms and cliffs
of power and helplessness, ice-lock
the free-running life of the mind. We move
in grandeur to the meltdown. There,
lines of a global banner hail us,
tell, in words we can no longer read,
the history of what we were.

In lowercase titter, agony columns
confide to the you, the me, that style
alone is serious. In darkness
we sneak to that Theater Schadenfreude
where, tied to the tracks, self-respect
in foolish ruffles and pantaloons
awaits the next episode. Romance,
whose feet in bed smell to high heaven,
is complained of by Constant Wife, while a-chill
in her trite Teddies, the Other Woman
poses outside to understand him.
Each morning ambition shaves off by finger
a lather of custard pie. Between
each feature the animated cartoon
of caritas as a permanent,
ridiculous adolescent plays.
When butterfingers drops the hot rock
of the heart from any ledge to the stream

of the life of the mind below, which goes up
in steam, then even Time's blind date
turns out to be a transsexual
and we all go home. There, on its forehead,
the artless mirror outlines our story:
There's no lifestyle for the feelings, yet
it's deathless, that trivial blazoning.

Double Sonnet for Minimalists

The spiral shell
apes creamhorns of smog,
Dalmation, quenelle
or frosted hedgehog,
yet is obsessed
by a single thought
that its inner guest
is strictly taught.

When the self that grew
to follow its rule
is gone, and it's through,
vacant, fanciful,

its thought will find
Fibonacci's mind.

That fragile slug,
bloodless, unborn,
till it knows the hug
of love's tutoring form,
whose life, upstart
in deep, is to learn
to follow the art
of turn and return,

when dead, for the dense
casts up no clue
to the infinite sequence
it submitted to.

May its bright ghost reach
the right heart's beach.

Sonnet for Minimalists

From a new peony,
my last anthem,
a squirrel in glee
broke the budded stem.
I thought, Where is joy
without fresh bloom,
that old hearts' ploy
to mask the tomb?

Then a volunteer
stalk sprung from sour
bird-drop this year
burst in frantic flower.

The world's perverse,
but it could be worse.

Firefall

1993

Addendum to "The Block"

"Three new babies are due all at once on the block,"
our soft-hearted widow tells us, walking her fat,
puffing poodle with a new pink bow on her ear.
"Two on the other side of the street, one here."

Within a week three front-step railings blossom
with pink or blue balloons and bold-faced signs
(commercial aids to displaying the shy new joy)
announcing that IT'S A GIRL or IT'S A BOY.

When one celebration comes down, it reveals a mourner.
A small, black dog runs up "to *everyone,*
all day," says the neighbor, and pleads for babying.
"Her nose is out of joint, poor little thing."

Soon, up and down both sidewalks, three black nannies
(two fat, one thin), each pushing a pristine carriage,
acquaint themselves with each other, paint high-pitched rainbows
of giggles and gossip over the street's doze.

The few old-timers, out for their therapeutic
heart-walks, glare or coo into a carriage
as suits their hearts: "More noise, clutter, *coping,*"
or "More life to wrap one's self in, breath, *hoping.*"

Before we know it, dangling by his wrist
from the hand of a leaning mother, one infant lurches
as far as our drive, legs testing this strange notion,
toes touching or missing the ground, eyes wild with promotion.

Much later a crowd chooses our street to parade
"ABORTION KILLS BABIES," their frozen faces
grim, their kids in strollers grim, as if we,
the human block, were beneath reality.

Firefall

Raked leaves in heaps lie at the curb for pickup.
Soon the cold will keep secret behind each door
pain, pleasure, vital, or lifeless conceptions,
boundless scopes or chilling circumscriptions.

This morning, though, the sun sends a wordless, warm
hug to us all—children, parents, barren
couples, frail graybeards, gays—"hello? goodbye?"
reaching out of the newborn blue of the sky.

The Marriage Sculptor

for Stephen and Mary

As we wandered, bored, in the halls of The Great Museum,
we came upon a late work of the sculptor
which made us stop and catch our breaths, so fine
the embrace of spirits, so expressive the bright pour

of leaning light, so rich the exchanging changes.
"One of his finest!" we all said, and brought
its image as souvenir to dangle before us.
In time, Time's tempests struck what had been wrought.

The piece, we saw, dispirited, was splintered
into wild beams that wildly searched through a dark
where changes lay in scatters. Then we saw
the sculptor, the old master, disembark.

Blind to us all, he turned his rapt face
to the wreck. "Safe. My materials, safe. All.
Now I must start my making. I see it—spirit,
light, change—more brilliant and powerful,

a larger work." Nothing human is perfect,
we thought. What can shelter the next from storm?
He spoke tenderly to his elements: "Beauty
learns from beauty, the first costly form

lies coiled in the last." Then, "I am not Eros.
Since Time is made out of it (who calls himself king)
the human stuff *I* work with is stronger than Time,"
he said to us, who thought we had lost something.

Poets in Late Winter

for Joe Summers
and Albert Lebowitz, birdwatchers

I

The poets of Missouri stare at astonishing winter.
On the windshields of their disabled cars they can see
rain, snow, hail, sleet, fog
all at once. Only the river still runs with pity.
The white sandwich they live on is snow between slabs of ice.
For three weeks no one can walk. Perhaps
sold-out salt will float in, they can sit beside
their stricken friend, iced in without guides or maps;
throw enough friction under their skidding souls
to pick up the news thrown on their own front yard
(One man who fell and lay helpless outside his door
clutched his paper and bellowed to wake his lifeguard,
who hunted the house up and down for her husband's voice);
can carry hot food to the trembling next-door widow
(self-immured for ten days from the poisonous glass)
without a steel-point stave to poke down to snow
while wearing golf shoes to crack-step across the lawn;
can send a serious verse to the humorist
who smashed her thirty-year-old hip. For three days
no mailman comes. Never was mail more missed.
Books and small-screen pall, poems that hail
into the cold mind coldly rattle like ping-pong.
In St. Louis seventy mailmen are hurt in falls
the day they try again. It goes on too long.

After two weeks the poets of Missouri hear
that their wintering-over birds are going to die.
For too long the inches of ice on top of snow
on top of ice have kept them from seeds, though they fly,

searching everywhere, through the freezing storms.
Each dried-berry-hung bush is iced off from a bill.
There is no water, each pond and stream stays solid.
Such innocent song to suffer the earth's ill-will!
In city, village, farm, frantic, the poets
set out to save the lovely reds and blues
of cardinal and jay, the cocky mocker,
junco, chickadee, waxwing . . . pulling their golf shoes
on and off all day, they balance warm water
again and again, fill feeders, their mittens smeared
with peanut butter, fat, raisins, breadcrumbs.
From wind and sorrow their face-scarves and eyes are teared.
And the little ones come from the woods, at least some, bedraggled,
too starved and thirsty to scare when food is thrown,
sparrows and starlings too, crows, pigeons, everybody.
Old bird books wake and call out birds unknown.
In his bright beret even the huge red-bellied
woodpecker hunches down to the holes of the feeders.
"If we stick together," he says to the poets of Missouri,
"the earth will reprint for its most devoted readers."

II

The poets of Missouri, in color, are dreaming
a T.V. drama that troubles their sleep:
when they sailed to these shores of being and seeming
they were met by a giant in exquisite motley
who became their faithful servant. Whatever
they asked he brought or did, though he
was mute except for a high little hum
(as he went about his magical work)
which they took to be happiness. Bang of drum
and now he appears, arms at his side,
dressed like a robot in Reynolds Wrap.
He is looking at them. Used to the big wide

billboards of human grief and desire,
they're unable to understand such a look.
Next a zoom to his heart. If he should aspire
to a heart, they supposed it crisp, firm, green
like a Granny apple. But what runny chaos
is this that erupts all over the screen?
Whatever it was is now worn, rancid,
its form weakened by lack of care,
lack of gratitude, praise. Amid
its weary, mushy straining to live
are runnels of need and pain. Their paper
feelings crumple as they cry, "Forgive . . ."
How *could* they have guessed that the generous monster
loved them? The camera shifts and he turns
transparent. Heart fills his throat like fur.
"Our word, our world," they cry, "we've been wrong!"
He tries to hum again, but chokes up
and ends that tiny, unearthly song.

Rascasse

In off-season chill, berthed yachts are spiking stems
into the plum-colored evening of the Harbor
outside the door. We attend our first authentic
bouillabaisse in Nice. On each table, *azur*
as the morning sea, a delicate white bouquet.
"What is that flower?" I ask the bowing blacktie,
his answer so startling I hear the English "I."
"Pardon? . . . oh, ail. Vraiment? C'est charmant ici!"
But we have not come for charm and blossom, but homeliness,
the deep, loamy musk of birth and decay
that hides from the eyes, the head of the garlic, the seed.

On the table rolled to ours a flat pan holds
the posed trio under a fiery arbor
of crabs, tails to a blue-black coil of conger.
On either side, like bridesmaids, the symmetry,
grace, sea-molded curves of mullet and loup;
in the center, the bride ("a first-class bouillabaisse
owes its quality to the *rascasse,* which is
essential"), *rascasse* the hog-fish, known to folk
and fishermen as the ugliest fish in the world.
Round, lovely eyes of her finny attendants
are blind to the rope of grotesque neck
that lifts a snouted face to her clan of lovers.

The surgeon-waiter bones with a click, click, click.
Over the flesh, divided and dealt, is poured
the broth of all, most prized for that one essence.

II

The eyes have led us astray through dreaming years,
cherishing consonance, curve, the colorful,
proportion, radiance, balance, harmony,
shapeliness that ages etched on our lenses.
We wed and bed the by-product, but spurn the essence.
We see the skin of the earth and it is beautiful,
but what formless fury fills earth's bowels and fuels us?
From Tennyson's "fire in the belly" sprang up poems.
Do the eyes want to look in the gut and know its essence?
From what came comfort of home, came fountain and spire?
From the mess of feeling, Yeats' "foul rag-and-boneshop."
What fertilizes but muck? What began us but slime?
We nod to the *belle-laide* with her troublesome half-truth,
but what gives comfort, what creates, but ugliness?

III

Suppose the light of the eyes went out and we walk
at a strange, cold moon's insistence into a place
bleached of curve, custom, and color, down ways
of misty shapelessness. We walk for days
(or nights). The world, if it is a world, is empty.
No shadow befriends us, our soles press spongy silence.
Finally on some street (or field or shore)
we come to an ugly house and enter. There
we feel, and smell the stench of, some boggy burning.
We kneel at the edge of it and hold out our hands.
Then slowly a center inside us begins to glow

through loops, knots, clumps, from head to toe,
dusky alleys, wires, bags, stems,
and rosy comfort flowers through every pore
into inconceivable gardens. Light flares on our lessons.
We have knelt at the unpraised heart of being, of essence.

IV

The rich broth of life, whose bubble eyes
hold both the unseen and the seen, will defend it—
essence—ugliness (eh, *rascasse?*), comfort.
May all the color and beauty of the world attend it!

Quotation from *French Riviera, Côte d'Azur,* Michelin Guide.

"We Are in Your Area"

At every hour of morning to night my telephone
brings me the news that they are in our area
(or will be in our area by the next afternoon),
Veterans of every war, in every condition
("Judith, you've *got* to get off that phone a half hour,"
a friend told her teenage daughter. "I'm expecting a call
from Disabled American Veterans!") vying to pick up
kindly old clothes that have learned our old bodies,
old dear castiron skillets, the old chairs
we sit on, re- and re-covered since the fifties,
all Lighthouses for the Blind, all Handicapped Workers
who truck in more, still more, Everlasting Light Bulbs,
brooms and mops for our bulging shelves and closets,
Spreaders of Cement Patios who would disembarrass
our yard of its big warm brick one, Tuckpointers, Roofers,
Vendors of the Latest Storm Window, Landscapers, Sweeps,
Construction and Remodelling groups in their urgent dozens
who would rip away our downstairs sideporch library
(where books of our friends nap in grownup silence
till we wake them up for a lively romp with our minds)
and nail on a family room for our long-lost children,
Cleaners of Carpets with Three-Room, Ten-Room Specials,
who disdain my expertise at pushing battered
sudsers and steamers rented from supermarkets,
Basement Waterproofers for our high, dry basement,
Driveway Glazers and Blacktoppers, Plasterers,
College Student Painting Services, pleading
to repaint the paint just spread by other such Students,
Tree Removers who would rid the birds and squirrels
of fruit and bloom I carefully planted and nurtured,
Lawn Care Specialists, scornful of amateur tending,
who poison, spray, feed, and aerate on schedule.

While my husband cleans the gutters of the next-door widow
I am on the phone being wooed by yearning guttermen.
There is such a jam in our area of ghostly vans,
pickups and flatbeds there's nowhere to park our car,
such milling crowds of phantom workmen in frontyards
and backyards one hardly dares to go out the door
and enjoy the garden or feed the birds, such parades
of strange, invisible machines being brought to the houses
one can scarcely walk the dog, one fears for the mailman.
Neighbors' houses are shielded away from a visit
by unseen flying buttresses of ladders.
And, in such a silent bedlam of roaring, smashing,
hacking, pounding, jackhammering, sawing, hissing,
in our area one can hardly hear one's self think.

II

But why aren't they in our area, why won't they come
when the furnace thermostat dies on the coldest weekend
of the whole winter, when a pipe rusts through and water
is pouring out of the ceiling, when treeroots squeeze
through the sewer pipe and grow into tangled clogs,
when all the lights in the neighborhood go out?
Without even a casual "See ya . . ." they have slipped away
to another area where they are all booked up.
And why have they left our area, those tender young boys
with the proud, serious faces of first-time earners,
who will mow the lawn, wash cars, try to do anything?
They have moved far away to full-blown adolescence,
to driving and dates, they will not come back anymore.
And why have they left, the long-time friends and neighbors
who moved many miles to country retirement homes
or to condos in far mushroom-bulging developments
which are hard to locate even with good directions?

And why, why, taking so much of ours with them,
have they left, those who always supplied us so freely
with our heat and light, those who drove clear off the maps
and left no directions? Soon we must set off to find
their precious, populous place, to be in their area.

Endings

for Howard Nemerov

I

Sometimes when I read a book (verse or memoir,
novel, tales, travel, fat or slim)
a collapsed balloon seeps silently under the door,
sucks me in, inflates, and is once more
the world itself, or the world in my favorite guise—
a sly, reckless, outrageous poet who rhymes
its fiddleheads with its frost ferns, its starspace
with pasture, buttes with gullies, Cloud Ears with cliff-face.
In an air filled with this unearthly Muzak
of earth, a child, eyes wide, is lifted and held
for a first sight by arms of the artistry
that found the view and breathes "Look!" The child is me.
Innocent of endings as anyone at an
Introduction, the rapt mind gazes, sees,
clasped, in love's murmur, in the world's strange song.
But the right hand's wiser senses, all along,
ripping through timelessness, have begun to measure.
Between a thumb and fingers the ground grows thinner,
begins to glow with an efflorescence like pain.
See slowly! I beg my eyes, but again and again
the fingers feel how fast the time is coming
when arms will drop, the child fall through and be gone.
Even more terribly, footnotes, index or postscript
can fool the alarm so the trap is abruptly tripped.
"I cannot bear it," I think, but read on in a rage
for the rest of whatever it is, for the child, for the "Look!"
until the hand on which my heart is depending
holds only the blank page that follows an ending.

11

Setting the VCR when we go to bed
to record a night owl movie, some charmer we missed,
we always allow, for unprogrammed unforeseen,
an extra half hour. (Night gods of the small screen
are ruthless with watchers trapped in their piety.)
We watch next evening, and having slowly found
the start of the film, meet the minors and leads,
enter their time and place, their wills and needs,
hear in our chests the click of empathy's padlock,
watch the forces gather, unyielding world
against the unyielding heart, one longing's minefield
laid for another longing, which may yield.
Tears will salt the leftover salad I seize
during ads, or laughter slow my hurry to pee.
But as clot melts toward clearness a black fate
may fall on the screen; the movie started too late.
Torn from the backward-shining of an end
that lights up the meaning of the whole work,
disabled in mind and feeling, I flail and shout,
"I can't bear it! I *have* to see how it comes out!"
For what is story if not relief from the pain
of the inconclusive, from dread of the meaningless?
Minds in their silent blast-offs search through space
—how often I've followed yours!—for a resting-place.
And I'll follow, past each universe in its spangled
ballgown who waits for the slow-dance of life to start,
past vacancies of darkness whose vainglory
is endless as death's, to find the end of the story.

For May Swenson

The world beside this one, imagination's egg,
rolls close to cuddle in our orbiting
(its shell impermeable to body or eye)
and inhales, like the feathered warmth of a spread wing
the forms that come forth fresh from their fiery making.

Tibetan Buddhists chant the names of things
"moonflower . . . shell . . . turquoise . . . mountain . . . sea"
to make "a perfect symbolic world . . . a world
reimagined . . . recreated,"* one that might be.
Out of a sprawling Mormon family,

riding a stick horse, the child, pug-nosed,
tow-haired, came to the place her life lay
deep in a slough of words and dredged there. Up
came the unheated shelter, the real name "May,"
the pride and peace of poems, their elegant play,

one warm and human love ("She was a true
hermit," Zan said) and all the beautiful furred,
winged, three-toed, four-toed, finned beings
that jewel the world. A belated grant assured
a year of "warmth and animals," the Great Bird.

Back home, she spent the morning on a poem,
playing with the young cat, scratching its cheek
to make it purr. Did she, above the purring,
hear the long-remembered *tick, tick, tick,*
the always miraculous signal of a beak?

Who knows? When a roughly star-shaped beam of light
from a chipped-out aperture blinded the wit

on the page, she put the cat and notebook down,
moved quietly to that shining, intimate
open place in the shell and entered it.

*Jennifer Atkinson, "Imagining the Ocean," *Threepenny Review.*

Mr. and Mrs. Jack Sprat in the Kitchen

"About half a box,"
I say, and the male
weighs his pasta sticks
on our postal scale.

To support my sauce
of a guesswork rhymer
he boils by the laws
of electric timer.

Our joint creation,
my searchings, revisions,
tossed with his ration
of compulsive precisions,

so mimics life
we believe it mandated
that God had a wife
who collaborated.

And cracked, scraped, old,
still the bowl glows gold.

Late Wishes

Scientific, I only
wished I'd wed an M.D.,
who could forecast the lonely
departure of Me.

But of late, realistic,
I think I'd much rather
have married the mystic
who predicts the weather.

Though the whimsical sky
toss down grim absolutes

with the proper supply
of bikinis or boots

a whole canton and I
could go out in cahoots.

Insiders

Within
the stout
a thin
wants out,

but a child
in the gray's
reconciled,
wants to stay,

so happy
to bicker
and win,

to be
in that thicker
skin.

Long Stretch

You were out of town
for the smashing surprise:
my head's heavy disguise
in a Pulitzer crown.

The massed flowers that poured in
spread a grave undertaking
on the word-wrestling ring
that my room's always been.

Well, why not? After all,
life's long contest, for us,
has turned strained, serious.
Close and closer the call.

On Olympus Art's mother
keeps her pet, place and show
hard to judge as a star,
but here, loving each other,
it's easy to know
who the real winners are.

The Beginning

The end
of passion
may refashion
a friend.

Eyes meet
in fear
of such dear
defeat.

The heart's core,
unbroken,
cringes.

The soul's door
swings open
on its hinges.

Miranda Grows Up

Prospero
foreknew
what snow
could do:
half-kill
the beguiled,
heart-chill
his child.

But she
forgave
what swirled

on every
brave
new world.

Closures

Line fourteen
closes
to serene
supposes.
A sparkling
soda
toasts the darkling
coda.

Life's canvas
only
would revoke

the lustrous,
lonely,
last stroke.

Falls

There, where I lived a quarter century, there was nothing
to look up for (oh, a perfect apple turning ripe
on one of the backyard trees, or a sudden new
birdnest), nothing ever in the sky but weather,
nothing for weather to do there but make corn
forever "knee-high by the Fourth of July."
Anger, resentment, self-pity, what were they
but weeds to be chopped out fast to make more room for the
crop, the only crop that rich land wanted.
Beauty in the soft backdrop of green hill-breasts
Grant Wood hung behind burned, bony faces?
If you saw that, then "You'd better get your head
on straight!" Only now can trained young eyes
who come from "away" utter in wonder, "He didn't
stylize a bit, he painted literally!"
Wildflowers were deadened into ragged dust-humps
at the edge of gravel roads whose stinging, blinding
clouds kept cars apart from one another.
Narrow, two-laned pavement let the corn
come marching in its stiff green to the very edge,
grudging the trail its ground. Our only travel:
a Sunday's forty gravel miles to dear Grandma's
village or Aunt's farm. Rarely, a Sunday
trip to Dad's folks, fifty miles to the Town
(those pious strangers who stiffly smiled at "little
Monna Jane," who never felt like me).
Rolling on paving between flat fields of green,
prized stalks, once or twice a frizzy yellow-green
of willows scribbled a wandering creek.
Sometimes there were miles of the stomach-heaving
stench of fields just fertilized with shit,
or cry of "Peeuuu! Skunk! Skunk got hit!"
and sometimes rising and falling above the cornrows
(like a waterfall of pure sound?) "Oh, Meadowlark!"

But what was a waterfall? It seemed to me
that more than "ocean" or "mountain" I wanted to see
the wonder-welling of a waterfall.
How could I ever have guessed my father's dream,
who never was vouchsafed his simplest thought?
A gangling high school junior, I was told
he'd bought a newfangled "trailer house" which, hitched
to our car, would waft us to the Western Sea.

Near dark the three of us stood with a crowd, looking up
from a hill off to the side of Yosemite's
great cliff where, after already blurred marvels
undreamed-of, my father's dream had brought us to be.
The top of the cliff was darker than the sky,
which slowly darkened to meet it till everywhere
was darkness of sky, the mind went dark, one stood
completely alone, breath held. It began: The Firefall.
Out of some secret opening in the sky
the first blazing streaks began to pour
toward earth, the rent in darkness widened and widened
to let fall a dazzling creek, then more and more
cascaded down the dark until a full
river of radiance from abstemious heaven
made its slow unbroken, quivering reach
for whatever bed on unknown ground would be given.
Who could have guessed from what some careless hand
had broadcast—those few tiniest, dimmest sparks
in the dark soil of the sky—that the sky was hiding
more brilliance than it could hint at, a hidden lark
whispered perhaps of things called symphonies.
How long was the Firefall? Time had kept its sands
from falling. What was the fire? Although it fell
from the soul's home and braided into its strands
of hue and heat that cool, unearthly white,
its glory poured from earth's burning body, red,
yellow, blue, orange, twining, twisting
to light, to stainless light. But no riverbed

lay below to lead it over the earth
and make its wonder a lasting link with heaven.
So close to heaven was the lip of the Fall, so light
the limbs that spun, locked, spun, even
so long and lovely was the fall toward solid ground
that, its parts one by one winking out in air
imperceptibly, the Firefall died from the very
breath of earth that begot its celestial flare.
On the ground below us no smoldering heaps glowed up.
Park lights went on. We walked home from the hill.
I walked toward what I had never before imagined,
hearing my own heart's life, its fill and refill.

"College? What's the good of your going to college?
No, I haven't got that kind of money!"
Months of tears. "All right, you get yourself
a scholarship to the State Teachers College,
come home on weekends—otherwise, no college."
Books! No classes in psychology
so I could learn what normal people were like,
but Books! Soon I got free run of the stacks,
the nice old ladies trying to teach classes
liked me and let me read. The god who wrote
poems and showed them to me gave me lists
of poets and novelists, called me a writer,
let me love-worship-adore him (first love
that lasted his life long), gave me one burning
kiss that changed the color of the sky,
left for a better job and wrote me heartfelt letters.
Weekends at home I read. "You've got to stop
that reading, it's going to make you lose your mind.
You're too big-headed already!" Refrain from Dad.
Two lasting hilarities: out of my lists
of authors I chose *Finnegans Wake* as a first
dip into Joyce. Grand-style bewilderment!
For first James I plucked *The Golden Bowl*
from the shelf, read with total pleased absorption,

reached the end, and only then woke up
to ask myself, "What in the world did I read?
What happened?" A new and lasting humility!
Poems I read by thousands rolled in my mind
like rocks, polished against each other, crumbling
to chips and dust only in late old age.
In summer before my sophomore year began
my father hitched the trailer up for the East.
Parked in the backyard of a relative
in calm New Jersey, we saw the World's Fair,
and, more to my poem's point, Niagara Falls.
Smirks from the relatives. "You know that's where
the honeymooners go? Well, guess it won't
be long before *you* go without your folks.
College girl, eh? Well, you'll get over that."

We walked toward a roar that reached beyond the senses.
No waterfall, it seemed, but earth's bringing together
of all its waters to make for that monstrous, open
mouth (one lip one country, one another),
out of a thousand long white quivering tongues
one tongue that brought from the depths of throat appalling,
thunderous boasts of its own fertility.
Unceasing, day and night, with its giant calling
shaking the shoulder we stood on with its passion,
the earth poured law to our puny selves, which shrank
to the size of a seed as in the roar of its will
it sucked from us our watery dross and drank.
"This is no waterfall for the newly wed,"
I knew within myself. "First the Firefall,
then, years later, here." We drove to see
the American lip from Canada's side, but the whole
was beyond the grasp of my lens and I snapped instead
a family of swans, a simpler sight,
father, mother, puffball babies, strolling.
At home I printed underneath in white
on the black album page, *Swans en Famille,*

proud of my first-year French. Prescient, perhaps,
but, with no course in Earth, I had read the roar.
"*Life!* Life and more life I want! Not *one* crop
but *thousands* in their unimaginable
abundance, shape, size, color, kind—*all*
the undreamed-of, the yet to come, my body will bear.
I tell my own truth in my waterfall."
Gradually we drove toward silence. Years
went by and a time came when I heard the roar
and eagerly bent my head to the waters' will
that filled my fleshy chambers to their core.
Wild for the blind, helpless confinement to send me
over the lip in a will-less fall, thrown
from my safe, observant stand, tossed, rammed,
broken, drowned perhaps—but love alone,
however strong and skilled, could build no barrel.
My field unamplified as the voice of one bird's
in the corn, I fall, rise, praise, fall,
sowing and tilling my single crop—Words. Words.

May one who comes upon a final book
and hunts in husks for kernel hints of me
find Niagara's roar still sacred to dim ears,
Firefall still blazing bright in memory.

The Delivery

I'm five. The petals of my timeless play
can unfurl while Mother hoes out other gardens.
The next-door child and I, alone with my toys,
confine to the dining room our discreet noise.
From the doorway: *"Betty, come here!"* The uprooted flower
falls dead with no warning. What had my friend done,
rolled a dimestore car over the table top,
stood on a chair to wave the little dustmop?
I will never know. She is tethered to Mother's hand
and Mother's voice begins the long scolding.
I start a soldier's march around and around
the table, stomping each foot to stomp out her sound.
Faster around I stomp until it is over,
Betty is gone and Mother takes hold of me.
"What's the *matter* with you? Why is your face so red?
Why, you're *crying,* your whole face is dripping wet!
Well, if that isn't silly, I'd like to know what is!
I wasn't scolding *you,* I was scolding *Betty.*"
She laughs. "Go wash your face." The room blears.
My hand wipes and finds all the unfelt tears.

Soon it is supper time. In the kitchen they feed
and talk, while I, invisible as I was
in high-chair days, silently sit on Sears,
wearing the weight of my big and bigger ears.
"Well, you'll never guess what your crazy kid did today—
if that wasn't the limit!" The story swells
into ache in my stomach, then Dad's laughter and hers
slice and tear like knives and forks and a worse
hurt is opening in my middle; in familiar
smells and muddle of voices, mashed potatoes,
dimming light, hamburger, thick creamed corn,
the milk-white chill, a self is being born.
And is swept away through seething clots of minnow

in the nearly hidden creek that weeps through the meadow,
smeared with mud from its suckling roots of willow,
to tributary, to river, deep and slow,
whose sob-like surges quietly lift her and carry
her unjudged freight clear to the mourning sea.
And there they are, all of the heavy others
(even Mother and Father), the floundering, floating or sinking
human herd, whose armstrokes, frail, awry,
frantic, hold up their heads to inhale the sky,
which gilds the tongues of water or soothes them to stillness
with white silk covers strewn with onyx and pearl.
She is with them, inept dog-paddler that she is.
The heavens whirl and drift their weightless riches
through streaky splendors of joy, or bare unending
lodes of blazing or ice-blue clarity.
With them all, all, she is scraped by crusted rock,
wrenched by tides untrue to heart or to clock,
fighting the undertow to shapelessness
in smothering deeps, to what is insufferable.
If those she can reach go under she cannot save them—
how could she save them? Omnipotent dark has seized them.
She can only sink with each one as far as light
can enter, meet drowning eyes and flesh still spangled
with tiny gems from above (a sign of the rare
her watered eyes never need), pointing to where,
up, in the passionate strain, lives everything fair
before she flails back to the loved, the illumined, air.

Notes to "Firefall"

1. The short poems in this book are minimalist sonnets along with a few I have baptized (oxymoronically, perhaps) extended minimalist sonnets.

Of all the forms, the sonnet seems most available to poets for deconstruction. Meter, rhyme scheme, division into octave and sestet, turn in thought, all have at one time or another been dispensed with by writers, and any poem of fourteen lines has been called a sonnet. In my own play with the form, I have shortened the conventional iambic pentameter line in varying degrees, some of the sonnets being held to a one-accent line; but I have kept all other conventions of the Shakespearean, Petrarchan, or Spenserian. The one convention that has remained constant through the years, the fourteen-line length, I have, however, occasionally broken by adding an extra four lines. I have found the shortened line and the additional quatrain (the extended minimalist sonnet) make for a form that is a pleasure to work with and—I hope—to read.

2. Because younger readers of "Falls" have been puzzled by what the firefall was, supposing it to have been the Northern Lights or some other natural phenomenon, a note may be useful. It was (in 1937, when I saw it, and as late as the 1950s, when a color photograph was taken) a nightly entertainment for tourists at Yosemite National Park, in which burning embers from what must have been an enormous bonfire were skillfully and continuously pushed over the top of a high cliff, creating in the dark a "waterfall" of fire. Anyone wishing to read a bit more about the Yosemite firefall is referred to *The Tourist at Yosemite, 1855–1985*, Stanford E. Demars, University of Utah Press, 1991.

Mona Van Duyn (Mrs. Jarvis Thurston) was born in Waterloo, Iowa, in 1921, grew up in Eldora, Iowa, and since 1950 has lived in St. Louis. She has taught at the University of Louisville and Washington University as well as at summer writing workshops: Breadloaf; Salzburg, Austria; in Texas, New York, Tennessee, Indiana, and Maryland. With her husband she founded *Perspective: A Quarterly of Literature* (1947) and co-edited it until 1967. She has received the National Book Award (1971), the Bollingen Prize (1970), and the Pulitzer Prize (1991) as well as several prizes from *Poetry,* including the Ruth Lilly Prize from that magazine, and an NEA Senior Fellowship. She is a member of the American Academy of Arts and Letters as well as the American Academy of Arts and Sciences, and was for fifteen years a Chancellor of the Academy of American Poets, having previously received its fellowship. Washington University, Cornell College, the University of Northern Iowa, George Washington University, Georgetown University, and the University of the South have awarded her the degree of Honorary Doctor of Letters. All of her work is in print at Knopf in three volumes: *If It Be Not I: Collected Poems 1959–1982* (1993), *Near Changes* (1990), and *Firefall* (1993). She was appointed by the Librarian of Congress to be Poet Laureate of the United States for 1992–1993.

A NOTE ON THE TYPE

This book was set in Adobe Garamond. Designed for the Adobe Corporation by Robert Slimbach, the fonts are based on types first cut by Claude Garamond (c. 1480–1561). Garamond was a pupil of Geoffroy Tory and is believed to have followed the Venetian models, although he introduced a number of important differences, and it is to him that we owe the letter we now know as "old style." He gave to his letters a certain elegance and feeling of movement that won their creator an immediate reputation and the patronage of Francis I of France.

Composed by Digital Composition, Berryville, Virginia
Printed and bound by Berryville Graphics, Berryville, Virginia
Designed by Virginia Tan